THE TABERNACLE OF ISRAEL

Its Structure and Symbolism
Illustrated

JAMES STRONG
Author of *Strong's Exhaustive Concordance*

KREGEL PUBLICATIONS
GRAND RAPIDS, MICHIGAN 49501

Tabernacle of Israel, by James Strong. New edition, completely revised and updated. Copyright © 1987 by Kregel Publications, a division of Kregel, Inc., P. O. Box 2607, Grand Rapids, MI, 49501. All rights reserved.

Illustrations: Don Ellens

Library of Congress Cataloging-in-Publication Data

Strong, James, 1822–1894.
  Tabernacle of Israel.

  Reprint. Originally published: The Tabernacle of Israel in the Desert. Providence, R.I.: Harris, Jones, 1888
  Includes indexes.
  1. Tabernacle. I. Title
BM654.S7   1987   296.4   85-8100
ISBN 0-8254-3745-8

  3 4 5 6 Printing/Year 91 90

Printed in the United States of America

CONTENTS

Illustrations

INTRODUCTION

For more than thirty years the subject of this work has been an earnest study with the author, and in the course of his investigation and comparisons he has procured and carefully examined every book of note treating upon it. The author has endeavored to unravel the entanglements which have hitherto baffled the skill and learning of interpreters and tried to make the whole of the tabernacle plain to the average comprehension. He has here brought together everything, thus far ascertained, that he judges adapted to be of service in conveying a just idea of that remarkable building, the first and (including its later development, the Temple of Jerusalem) the only one immediately devised and directly authorized by the Almighty Himself as His place of special worship for His chosen people. As such it has ever since held a conspicuous position in the eyes and thoughts of saints, and in these days of archaeological science it has still retained its hold upon the reverent curiosity of an intelligent world. Great pains have been taken by learned men to restore it as fully as possible to the understanding of modern Occidentals. The present effort, it is hoped, will not be regarded as overambitious in aspiring to do this more completely than heretofore for popular purposes. The author has no pet theory to establish, nor any doctrinal influence to bias him. He has simply attempted to collect, weigh and combine the information afforded by every source accessible, to incorporate whatever new features his own discoveries and comparisons have introduced, and to present everything really pertinent in as lucid and systematic a form as the topic allows.

AUTHORITIES ON THE TABERNACLE

There are a number of authorities that have written on the Tabernacle.

The most trustworthy, as well as the fullest and most definite source of information concerning the Israelitish Tabernacle is, of course, the Bible, especially the classic passage of Exodus 25-28, which minutely prescribes the construction of the edifice and its apparatus, together with the parallel passage of Exodus 35-40, which describes, in almost the same words, the execution of the task. The phraseology of the original record, although remarkable for its terseness, will be found, when minutely examined, to convey or to imply precisely enough to guide the reader in every important particular.

Considerable additional light is thrown upon the subject by the specifications later made in the scriptural account of the Temple of Solomon (1 Kings 6; 2 Chron. 3, 4), including that seen in vision by Ezekiel (40-42), both of which were modeled, in all their most essential features, after the plan of the Tabernacle, as we shall have occasion to see. Scattered notices are occasionally given elsewhere in the Scriptures, which serve to confirm, complete, or correct our inferences from these main fountains of specification.

Of profane authorities in ancient times the principal one by far is Flavius Josephus,[1] who in his well-known description of the earliest sacred building of the Jews, repeats, with some variation and a few original suggestions, the statements of the Scriptures on the subject.

Very little information is contained in the rabbinical writings of the Jews, which could aid us in reconstructing the Tabernacle, and none at all in the literature of any heathen nation of antiquity, except the Egyptians, whose temples were evidently a type, but only in the most general sense, of the Tabernacle and the Temple. For although both these edifices were expressly planned by the divine Architect (Exod. 25:40; 1 Chron. 28:11, 12, 19), yet the triple

---

1. Flavius Josephus, *Antiquities of the Jews,* III, vi, 2-vii, 7. This work and *Wars of the Jews* can be found in *The Complete Works of Josephus* (Grand Rapids: Kregel Publications).

arrangement of a shrine within a sanctuary, and this again within an outer enclosure, was a marked feature of the noted temples with which the Hebrews had become familiar in Egypt. It is true that these structures, the remains of which have survived to the present day, were built at a much later date than that of the Exodus, but they are doubtless successors of earlier edifices resembling them in their main outlines.

In a similar way the sacerdotal regalia of the ancient Egyptians, and their sacrificial implements, as depicted upon their monuments, give us a partial clue to the intricacies of some of the Jewish priestly services and garments, especially that curious article called the *ephod,* and its mysterious accompaniments. (See Fig. 34.) Likewise the sacred Ark, with the cherubic figures upon it, is illustrated to some extent in the hieratic boat sketched on the sculptures as borne in procession by the Egyptian priests, and then deposited in the *adytum* of their temple. (See Fig. 26.) Assyriology also furnishes a few hints as to some particulars.

From a most unexpected quarter there has come a clear ray to determine some of the vexed questions concerning the utensils of the Tabernacle, especially the Golden Candelabrum. Delineations of the successors of these objects, taken by the Romans on the fall of Jerusalem, appear upon the memorial arch of Titus at Rome and are the more valuable, as being undoubtedly authentic and carved by contemporaries. (See Fig. 1.) They are probably more elaborate, as was true of all the apparatus in the Herodian Temple, than those in the Solomonic structure, and still more so doubtless than the severe style of the earlier Tabernacle; yet they serve a most important use in deciding where particulars are elsewhere lacking or uncertain. These specimens were copied by the indefatigable A. Reland in the eighteenth century, when they were perhaps less dilapidated than now; and his drawings were printed in his learned monograph on the subject (*De Spoliis Templi,* etc., Utrecht, 1716). (See Figs. 20, 22.) This little work of Reland, like all his other archaeological investigations, is well-nigh exhaustive of the special topic on which it treats, so far as information was attainable in his day. The present appearance of the Arch of Titus is shown with photographic exactness in many published volumes, and the actual remains are open to the inspection of every tourist.

Oriental usages, which, although ascertained chiefly by modern travellers, are of so permanent a character that they may fairly be ranked with antiquarian researches, aid us to a great extent in forming an accurate conception of the Tabernacle and its appliances.

Writings of our own time[2] are, of course, secondary in their authority on such a subject as this, but they cannot safely be ignored. On the contrary the wise and candid archaeologist will welcome and carefully weigh every new suggestion of other minds, earnestly devoted to the solution of the many problems still undeniably left on these difficult particulars. He may not, indeed he cannot, accept all their conclusions, for they often widely conflict with one another, and not infrequently contradict plain inferences from the language of the ancient record, or probable necessities of the case.

Among the works of a general antiquarian character, that bear specially upon this topic, we mention, as probably the most important, K.W.F. Bähr's *Symbolik des Mosaischen Cultus* [Symbolism of the Mosaic Worship] (2 vols., 1837-39), which, with much learning and judiciousness, discusses most of the architectonic as well as symbolic questions relating to the Jewish Tabernacle (i, 56), and has been the chief treasure-house for more recent explorers in the same line. Of later treatises expressly on the Jewish Tabernacle as a whole, I want to mention the following titles: *The Holy Vessels and Furniture of the Tabernacle* and *The Tabernacle, the Priesthood and the Offerings* by Henry W. Soltau.[3] They are splendid volumes and altogether popular in their character.

---

2. Until 1888, when this work was first published.

3. Published by Kregel Publications, Grand Rapids, Michigan. The author also mentioned a number of other works on the Tabernacle, but as they are all out-of-print and mostly in foreign languages, we have not included them in this edition.

CHAPTER 1

HISTORY OF THE TABERNACLE

It appears in Exodus 33:7 that the name "Tabernacle of the Congregation"[1] was originally applied to an ordinary tent, probably the one officially occupied by Moses himself; and that this was at first set apart by the token of the divine presence at its doorway as the regular place of public communication between Jehovah and the people. (See Fig. 14.) This was prior to the construction of what was afterwards technically known as the Tabernacle, which of course superseded such a temporary arrangement.

Soon after the arrival of the Israelites in the center of the Sinaitic mountains, Moses was directed by Jehovah to prepare a special building for his worship, according to a pattern shown him during his stay of forty days on the summit of the mount. Accordingly, orders were immediately issued for contributions to this end, the materials were freely offered by the people, a chief artificer, "Bezaleel, the son of Uri, the son of Hur, of the tribe of Judah," with

---

1. The Hebrew phrase here employed is *óhel möéd* (lit. "tent of meeting") which, however, is often used synonymously with *mishkán ha-edúth* (lit. "dwelling of the assembly") to designate the edifice itself. Strictly speaking, the terms "tent" (*óhel*) and "tabernacle" (*mishkán*) are found to be carefully discriminated (as we shall eventually see), denoting respectively the canvas roof and the wooden walls of the compound structure; never for both, except as the one implies the other; and absolutely never for each other. The expression, "tent of meeting" (often falsely rendered "tabernacle" in the A.V.), is especially appropriate from the fact that the representatives of the congregation of Israel were required to assemble for the divine commands at the "opening" (Heb. *péthach,* A.V. "door") of the *tent;* for there was no *mishkán* or wooden part at the front of the building.

"Aholiab, the son of Ahisamach, of the tribe of Dan," as his assistant (Exod. 31:2, 6), was selected to have immediate charge of the task. After about eight months' labor, the Tabernacle, with all its equipments, was completed and erected on the first day of the first month (Nisan) of the second year after the departure from Egypt (Exod. 40:17). The cloudy Pillar of the divine Shekinah doubtless indicated the precise spot of its location by resting over the central object of the entire worship, the sacred Ark beneath the Mercy Seat. During the journeys and the halts in the wilderness, as well as throughout the campaigns in Moab, the Tabernacle marked the headquarters of the Israelitish host, and on the arrival in Canaan it accompanied Joshua in most of his expeditions against their enemies. In all of these migrations it was taken down piecemeal, carried on vehicles constructed for the purpose and drawn by oxen, in charge of the priests assisted by the Levites, and was reerected at every stopping place. The position of the several tribes of Israelites was regulated by divine prescription around it, both on the march and in the encampment, the signal for starting or halting being the motion or the resting of the mute guide, the Pillar cloudy by day and fiery by night. As a slowly-burning pyre (Exod. 3:2) it shows white—like smoke in the daylight, but red—like flame at night. Occasionally (Exod. 14:20) it was dark on one side, and bright on the other.

In the latter part of Joshua's administration, the Tabernacle was set up at Shiloh (Josh. 18:1), where it remained during the troubled period of the Judges, down to the days of Eli,[2] when the sacred Ark was taken out of the building (1 Sam. 4:4), and never returned. It is probable that the timber of the wooden part of the edifice (the curtains, of course, having been often renewed) was by this time so worn and decayed (although of durable wood and thickly plated with gold) as to be unserviceable, and Talmudic tradition speaks of its replacement by a permanent stone structure, traces of which, it is thought, are still discoverable on the site of Shiloh. However that may be, there are no further distinct indications of the existence or

---

2. From the narrative in 1 Samuel 3, it would seem that the original court was replaced or at least occupied by permanent dwellings for the ministrant priests.

locality of the original building, although evidences occur of the transfer of the worship, under Samuel's administration, successively to Mizpeh (1 Sam. 7:6), and elsewhere (1 Sam. 9:12; 10:3; 20:6; Ps. 132:6). In David's day the shewbread was at one time kept at Nob (1 Sam. 21:1-6), which implies the existence there of at least one of the sacred utensils of the Tabernacle; especially as the priests largely lived there (22:11), and some part of their residence appears to have served, in so far at least, the purpose of a sanctuary (21:7, 9). Even down to the close of David's reign the "high place that was at Gibeon" possessed some fragments of the original Tabernacle, with its altar of burnt offering (1 Chron. 16:39; 21:29; comp. 1 Kings 3:4; 2 Chron. 1:3-6). This is absolutely the last mention of the edifice itself.

Meanwhile a rival establishment to the last one named had been set up by David on Mt. Zion at Jerusalem, whither he had finally transported the sacred Ark,[3] and gathered around it the sacerdotal ministrations in a new sanctuary, especially constructed for it, but which, as it is simply called a *tent* (1 Chron. 15:1; 16:1; 2 Sam. 6:17, "tabernacle"), would seem to have lacked the wooden walls of the earlier one (2 Sam. 7:2; 1 Chron. 17:1). (See Fig. 14.) This of course was in turn superseded by the famous Temple not long afterwards erected by Solomon, into which was doubtless gathered all that remained of the original furniture of the Mosaic Tabernacle (2 Chron. 5:5). The Candelabrum, however, if still extant, was replaced, in this edifice, by ten others, probably of a more gorgeous style (1 Kings 7:49), with at least a repeating of the altar of incense and the Table of Shewbread (1 Kings 7:48). The Laver, having probably long since been broken up, was also magnificently re-

---

3. This central object of the Jewish worship, after its seven months' adventures among the Philistines (1 Sam. 6:1) under Eli, had been deposited at Kirjath-jearim (1 Sam. 7:1), where it remained twenty years (v. 2) until Samuel's establishment at Mizpeh (v. 6). After its removal by David, first from Kearjath-jearim (where by some means it had got back meanwhile apparently by way of Bethlehem [comp. Ps. 132:6; 1 Sam. 9:14] to the house of Obed-edom, and afterwards to Jerusalem (2 Sam. 6, 1 Chron. 13—16), we have no record of its leaving the Holy City, except for a few hours on the breaking out of Absalom's rebellion (2 Sam. 15:24-29).

placed (1 Kings 7:23,27). On the demolition of the Temple by Nebuchadnezzar's general, such pieces of the sacred furniture as had survived all previous changes and catastrophes probably shared the fate of the other valuables there, being all carried away to Babylon (Jer. 52:18,19), whither some articles of the kind had already preceded them (2 Chron. 36:7). There they remained till the downfall of that city (Dan. 5:2,3), when the conqueror, Cyrus, delivered them to the Jewish "prince of the exiles" (Ezra 1:7-11). They were among the treasures soon afterward permitted to be transported to Jerusalem (Ezra 5:14,15; 7:19), where they safely arrived under Ezra's administration (Ezra 8:33). They seem at this time, however, to have consisted exclusively of the smaller but very numerous "vessels" for sacred uses, and no mention is made, in any of these later enumerations, of the Ark or the more important pieces of furniture. Evidences of a tradition appear in much later Hebrew literature to the effect that, on the capture of Jerusalem, or perhaps rather its final despoliation, the Ark was hidden away by Jeremiah, to be restored only on his return with the final dominion of Israel; but this is doubtless unfounded. The precious palladium of the Holy City (1 Sam. 4:3) seems to have attracted the cupidity of some one of the foreign or domestic marauders who at various times violated the sanctity of the shrine (2 Kings 12:18; 18:16; 2 Chron. 25:24; 28:24) down to the period of the Babylonian invasion (2 Kings 24:13). There is distinct mention of the Table of Shewbread in the reign of Hezekiah (2 Chron. 29:18), and, in that of Josiah, allusion is perhaps made to the autograph copy of the Law originally deposited in the Ark (2 Chron. 34:15). After this date all direct traces of any of the sacred apparatus constructed in the desert vanish from history. The few extra-biblical notices of the furniture of the Herodian Temple, some pieces of which may possibly have been the same as those of the Tabernacle, will be considered in treating of their original construction. (See Chap. 3.)

CHAPTER 2
THE STRUCTURE
OF THE TABERNACLE

In this chapter, our aim will be to explain as succinctly as possible the various parts of the sacred edifice and their adaptation to each other, chiefly from the Scripture record, accompanied by suitable diagrams, without entering into any unnecessary controversy of the opinions of others who differ from us as to the proper mode of reconstruction. Our chief purpose throughout is not simply to justify our own delineation, but rather to aid the reader in his conception and apprehension of it. If it shall then appear consistent, it will be its own best vindication.

The sacred narrative begins with a *pre*scription of the central object of sanctity, the Ark, and proceeds outward to the less holy precincts; but, as ours is a *de*scription, we pursue the reverse order, in accordance with modern methods. The inspired writer develops his subject from an interior point of view, but common mortals can only look upon it from without.

THE COURTYARD

The Court was a space enclosed around the Tabernacle itself in the midst of each camping ground, for the exclusive use of the priests and Levites in their sacred ministrations, and it was always so arranged as to face the East. The first encampment on which it was laid out was of course immediately in front or north of Mt. Sinai, where the fine plains of Er-Râhah stretches on an average a mile and one half wide and about three miles long—besides its continuation, through side-valleys to the very foot of the majestic hills on all sides towering about 3,000 feet sheer above it. The central peak, directly opposite, is now called Ras Sufsâfeh (*Willow Top,* from a small tree of that kind in a cleft of its summit), and is doubtless the very spot—plainly visible in the clear atmosphere to the whole camp at its base—where the Law was delivered amid flashes of lightning; while the rear peak—somewhat higher, but hidden at this point of view by its forward fellow—is still designated as Jebel Mûsa (*Moses's Mount*), being no doubt that on which the Hebrew lawgiver held his prolonged interview with Jehovah.

This outer and only court of the Tabernacle was 100 cubits long and 50 wide (Exod. 27:9,12,18), or reduced to English measure,[1] an oblong of about 172 by 86 feet.

1. We may here state, once for all, that our estimate of the length of the Hebrew cubit, in this book, is the same as that finally adopted by the late celebrated Egyptologist, Sir John Gardner Wilkinson, namely, 20.625 inches or 1.719 feet (*Ancient Egyptians,* ii, 258). This substantially agrees with the following ancient specimens of the cubit still extant, which the author has personally examined and measured.

Nilometer at Elephantine (average) .... 20.627 inches
Copper Rule in Turin Museum .... 20.469 inches
Wooden Rule in Turin Museum .... 20.563 inches
Stone Rule in Turin Museum .... 20.623 inches

The Turin copper cubit rule has evidently shrunk in cooling from the mold in which it was cast. The wooden one may have worn away somewhat. The stone one is rather irregular at the edges of the ends. The cubits marked on the stairway at Elephantine differ considerably from each other. Other cubit rules exist varying, according to published measurements, from 20.47 to 20.65 inches. An approximation to the exact standard is all that can now be determined.

The above cubit rules at Turin, together with others preserved in the various museums of Europe and elsewhere, have been carefully delineated and analyzed by R. Lepsius (*Die alt-ägyptische Elle und ihre Eintheilung,* Berlin, 1865), who estimates the ancient Egyptian full cubit, from these specimens and a comparison of the dimensions of the Pyramids (presumed to be in even cubits, as given by ancient writers, and proportional, both outside and in), as equivalent to one foot and $8\frac{1}{3}$ inches English, or very slightly in excess of the conclusion adopted by us. (The paper, however, on which they are printed has shrunk in drying from the lithographic press, so that they are three-eights of an inch shorter than the actual length. This is confirmed by the fact that he computes the entire cubit, on this

The Pillars

The Court area was enclosed by a curtain or hanging, of corresponding length, suspended upon pillars five cubits high (Exodus 27:18). These fence posts, as we would call them were doubtless of acacia ("*shittim,*" sing. "*shittáh*"), like the other wooden portions of the edifice, and probably round, as their type in nature (a tree), and economy of weight for a given degree of strength, seem to require. We may safely estimate their diameter at one fourth of a cubit, or about five inches. Like the other columns of the building, they appear to have been of the same size from top to bottom. Their foot was held in place by a socket or plate[2] of copper (A.V. incorrectly

same plan, at 525 *millimètres,* i.e., 20.65 inches.) That the Hebrew cubit was the same, can hardly be questioned. The Egyptian cubit rule was divided into 28 equal *digits* (finger-breadths), the first 15 of which were graduated into fractional parts (from the half to the sixteenth respectively). Four digits made a *palm* (hand-breadth, exclusive of the thumb); three palms made a *small span,* or three and a half a *large span,* four palms a *foot,* five palms an *elbow* (from the wrist), six palms a *short* (or, "moderate," i.e., medium-sized person's) *cubit* (including the length of the palm only), and seven palms the "royal," i.e., full-sized man's) *cubit,* from the tip of the middle finger to the elbow, i.e., the entire lower arm. Thus each of the parts, as well as the whole, was determined by a natural type (Rev. 21:17). These subdivisions were regularly numbered from right to left, and most of the surfaces were embellished with emblematical and mythological hieroglyphics. The favorite shape was that of a flat rule with one edge beveled, the digit marks being incised on most or all of the faces, and the fractions on the thin edge. None are jointed, for folding. The distinction last noted, namely, between the scant and the normal cubit, seems to explain the remark in Ezek. 43:13, "The cubit is a cubit and an hand-breadth," i.e., the full cubit, and not the short one, is intended (so in Ezek. 40:5).

2. The Hebrew word (Exod. 27:10-18) is *éden,* "a base," used also of the similar underpinning (as we shall see) of the Tabernacle walls, and elsewhere only of the foundation of the earth (Job 38:6), or the pedestal of a statue (Song of Sol. 5:15). The weight of the superstructure, or a slight excavation, would settle these somewhat into the ground, and thus prevent the foot of the entire structure from sliding. The old fashioned idea (apparently corrected under the rendering "socket"), that they were hollow pointed receptacles, is an utterly impracticable one, because they could not have been driven accurately (to fit the tenons) in the hard gravelly and stony soil of the desert. They would soon have been battered to pieces; nor would they have been of any use, since the tenons themselves might as well have been pointed, and driven in at once.

"brass," for zinc, which is used in that alloy, was unknown to the ancients),[3] evidently laid flat upon the ground, doubtless with a mortice or hole (probably square, in order to prevent the pillar from revolving) in the center, to receive a corresponding (copper) tenon in the end of the pillar. They were stayed upright by cords (Exod. 35:18) fastened to pins (27:19)[4] of copper driven into the ground, which would be necessary both on the inside and on the outside. The curtains with their attachments (especially the rods presently to be considered) would keep the tops at a proper distance apart, and the corners would brace the whole line. There were sixty of these pillars in all, namely, twenty on each side, and ten on each end, with an equal number of sockets (vv. 10-12). This allows exactly five cubits' space between the pillars (from center to center), the corner pillars, of course, being counted only once (and set half their thickness nearer the adjoining ones), whether in the side or the end.

This disposition of the pillars, which is the modern workmanlike method in dealing with fence posts, harmonizes the numbers and dimensions of the sacred narrative, and meets all the proprieties in the case. The question raised as to the mode of reckoning is a mere dispute about words, which has led some to make more and some less than sixty posts, and many to assign fractional and even different spaces between them. The exact truth is that the corner posts belong one half to the side and one half to the end (and so of the doorway posts and their wings), so that the language of the sacred writer is strictly corect. In counting the pillars of the respective sides of the rectangle and those of the doorway, both extremes are neither

---

3. The monuments show that the ancient Egyptians were familiar with the processes of metallurgy, and the mines of Surabet el-Khadim, in the desert of Sinai, are known, from old papyri, as well as the *débris* and inscriptions in the vicinity, to have been worked by them from a very early period. It is probably to these operations that the book of Job (chap. 28) refers, a work which Moses himself, who doubtless often witnessed the miners during his exile in Midian, is believed to have edited. The copper was smelted, no doubt on the spot, from the malachite there obtained. There would, therefore, be no difficulty in the Israelites effecting these castings at Sinai.

4. The Hebrew word is *yéther,* everywhere used of a tent pin. It was probably round and pointed, with a head or notch to keep the cord from slipping off.

included nor both excluded, but (as every one's experience must have taught him to do in such cases) one is included and the other excluded. A careful inspection of both accounts (Exod. 27:9-16; 38:9-19) shows that the number of the pillars is never predicated of the *sides* of the court, but always either of the court itself or (usually) of the *hangings;* and so likewise not of the opening of the doorway, but of its screen. This justifies the phraseology, inasmuch as the curtains, being continuous, would count (so to speak) the *spaces* rather than the pillars which they represented. Or perhaps we may more clearly apprehend the reason of this mode of reckoning, if we bear in mind that it was prescriptive and constructive, and not as erected; the materials being indicated—so many pillars prepared for such a length of curtain, care being taken not to duplicate or omit anything. The execution of the directions was left to the common sense of the workmen, and the interpreter has need to exercise his own in the exposition. We will find a similar enumeration employed, for the sake of uniformity, in the loops attached to the exterior curtains of the building; and Matthew 1:17, may be cited as an analogous case.

That the above interval is the true one is rendered certain by the length of the doorway curtain, twenty cubits for four pillars (27:16; 38:18,19), as well as by that of each of the side-curtains, fifteen cubits for three pillars (27:13, 14; 38:14, 15), thus making up the entire end of fifty cubits for ten pillars (27:12, 13; 38:12, 13). The corner pillars of the doorway are not counted twice, although both the colored and the plain curtains hung on them; but, precisely as in the case of the corner pillars of the court, where the two sections of curtains meet, they are accurately attributed one half to either side of the dividing line in their middle. This is the only way in which the doorway can be brought in the center of the front, as it evidently was meant to be. There were clearly ten *spaces* of five cubits each, from the centers of the pillars severally. Any other distribution is complicated and unnatural. In fact, aside from the question of the regularity of spacing, the only consistent and uniform method of counting the pillars possible is to include in each enumeration one of the means, but not the other. If both be included, there will really be but ninety-eight around the whole court, since two of the corners must be counted twice; or, if both extremes be excluded, there will be 104 in all, since the four corners must be left out altogether; similarly on the front, if both extremes be included on the entire line, as well as at the entrance, there will be but eight in all; or if both be excluded there will be twelve. Paine arbitrarily assumes that both extremes are to be included in the sides of the court, but excluded from the ends; yet he is compelled to include one extreme only in the side curtains of the front end.

Accordingly, the eastern or front end is said to have four such spaces in the middle for a doorway (twenty cubits wide), and three spaces or fifteen cubits on either side of these (vv. 14-16). From the parallel passage of Exodus 38:17,19 we learn that all the pillars were capped with silver, probably a curved plate to protect the top. Two other parts or appendages to these pillars are mentioned, namely, "hooks" and "fillets," both of silver (vv. 10, 12, 17). The former of these[5] obviously were to serve the purpose of holding up the other parts of the screen, and the latter[6] can only be a *rod,* not designed to sustain the curtain by means of loops or rings in its top edge, no

---

5. Hebrew *vav,* the name of the sixth letter of the alphabet, formed thus, ⟨, which indicates the shape of the hook or peg, being driven horizontally into the pillar. It was probably made of wire, or at all events round. T.O. Paine (for a reason apparent below) figures the antique style of the letter (adopting this form, Ⴤ), but this will make little difference, for in old inscriptions it appears in forms not essentially different from the above printed shape. (For example, on the Moabitic stone quite as often thus, Ⴤ , and in the very earliest specimen hitherto discovered, namely the Siloam inscription, exclusively thus ⟨, which is substantially the same as on old coins, thus ×.)

Fig. 2.—Pillar, with rods and hooks

6. Hebrew *chasúk,* something "fastened," i.e., a pole; used only of this object, and a word of similar form *chishshúk,* of the spoke (A. V. "felloe") of a wheel (1 Kings 7:33). As the rods of the Tabernacle doorway were overlaid with gold (Exod. 36:38), and were consequently not solid metal, but only a wooden pole encased (like the bars of the planks to be presently considered), these silver rods were probably constructed in a similar manner. The eyes at their extremities for the hooks must have been driven into their ends. Paine inserts the hooks upright in

such contrivances being anywhere mentioned in the text (as they invariably are whenever used. They were intended to keep the tops of the posts at a proper distance apart, being hung upon the hooks, apparently by means of eyes at each end (these last implied in the statement of their corresponding hooks, just as mortices in the sockets are taken for granted to fit the tenons of the posts and planks). The hooks were set one each in the middle of the round face of the pillar a little below the cap, and probably another near the bottom (See Fig. 2.) The stay ropes on either side might readily be fastened around the top of each pillar by a hitching noose in the middle, which the hooks would keep from slipping down.

The curtains thus hung upon the pillars were sheets of "fine twined linen,"[7] of unusual body and brilliancy, probably sewed endwise together so as to form a continuous screen from the doorway all around the corners to the doorway again. This would most conveniently be hung on the outside of the pillars, and being five cubits wide (Exod. 38:18),[8] it would clear the ground, if stretched smooth by eyelets in the upper and lower edges for the hooks. The doorway curtain, twenty cubits long, in the middle of

---

the tops of the pillars, and hangs the curtains upon the rods; but this arrangement, by drawing the curtains partly around the pillars, shortens them and prevents their hanging smooth. We shall also see that it will not apply to the description given of the inmost screen, called "the veil" by way of eminence. The etymology of the words is no objection to placing the hooks horizontally, any more than the knobs.

7. Hebrew *shesh moshzár,* lit., "white twisted" cloth, i.e., bleached material of two-stranded thread, doubtless of flax. *Shesh* seems to denote any very white substance, and is applied even to marble (Esth. 1:6; Song of Sol. 5:15). The proper word for linen is *bad,* which as distinguished from *shesh* would be the unbleached stuff of its natural color. The fineness of the thread is not involved in either term.

8. From this passage it appears that all the curtains around the court were of the same height. The singular expression there used, "The height in the breadth," means that the height was occasioned by the width of the cloth, which ran horizontally. In the arrangement which we have adopted, all the rods (or *rails* we might call them) for this fence are of the same length, inasmuch as they are carried entirely across the corner posts, and these latter are set wholly within the line. It is only necessary to have the single hook in these posts (at the extreme angle of course) not driven in so far into the post, i.e., projecting farther from its face.

the eastern end, however, was a different kind of stuff, "blue, and purple, and scarlet, and fine twined linen, wrought with needle-work" (v. 16), i.e., as we were the first to interpret it, the warp (or lengthwise threads) of bleached linen cord, and the woof (or filling) of alternate bars (running as upright stripes) of wool dyed blue-purple (violet),[9] red-purple (Tyrian),[10] and crimson (cochineal),[11] with hand-embroidery superimposed.

It should be noticed that in neither case is the substance, of which these two parts of the fabric was composed, explicitly mentioned. (Cf. the enumeration of the same materials first in 25:4.) That it was first woven in a loom, and afterwards worked with a needle, is obvious. Besides this the different colors only are named. The "bleached" was the basis, that is, the warp, as being the stronger, and for this purpose "double-twisted." That it was linen is to be inferred from the fact that it was bleached. On the other hand wool only will take rich colors well, especially animal dyes (the two purples are from shellfish, and the bright red from an insect). The cross bands of these three shades of red (as we may style them) would be softened by the admixture of the white foundation. On these the embroidering was performed, as the contrast would thus be very effective. The color of the embroidery would, we presume, be yellow, of silk thread, we suppose (as gold is not mentioned here), apparently on the "right" or outer side only. The figures do not seem to have been cherubim, as these are mentioned in connec-

---

9. Hebrew *tekéleth,* the *helix ianthina,* a very thin, flat and coiled, round shell, found on the Mediterranean, the envelope of a colorless, jelly-like animal, which when crushed or punctured emits a beautiful violet liquid.

10. Hebrew *argamán,*the *murex brandaris,* a large spiral shell, found in the Mediterranean, a particular part of the animal inhabiting which contains a creamy fluid, that turns a brilliant purple after exposure to the air.

11. Hebrew *shaní,* often with the addition of *toláath,* a *worm* or grub; the *coccus ilicis,* a parasite on the Tyrian oak, the wingless female of which furnishes the *kermes* of commerce, and yields a rich red color, very closely resembling that of the *coccus cacti* or true cochineal (which came from Mexico), being somewhat less brilliant but more permanent.

tion with the inner tapestry only, where they would be more appropriate. We are forbidden by the second commandment (although not yet promulgated) to think of any actual object, and must therefore conjecture that the needlework consisted of purely fancy patterns, such as abound in Oriental tapestries, ceilings and rugs—perhaps what is known as "mosaic." The order of the colors, as systematically named, leads us to conceive that the violet stripe was first, the purple in the middle and the crimson last, the white underneath and the yellow over the whole. The three primary colors (blue, red and yellow) are thus represented, but not in their prismatic order. The symbolism is of a less scientific nature, as we shall eventually see. The rainbow has its own symbolism (Gen. 9:12-16), but it is entirely cosmical. Josephus suggests[12] that the *linen was the warp*, but he says nothing about the woof, nor the order of the colors; he seems to have thought these were only used for the embroidery: "It [the high-priest's robe] is embroidered with flowers of scarlet, and purple, and blue [reversing the colors], and fine-twisted linen; but the warp was nothing but fine linen".

From their mode of attachment it is clear that none of these curtains (not even that of the doorway, which is explicitly stated to have been a single piece) were intended to be parted or to slide for admission; entrance could therefore only be effected by lifting them at the bottom and passing under them (as they were 5 cubits, or more than $8\frac{1}{2}$ feet, high), and this moreover was not possible with any degree of facility (on account of the tightness of the long lines) except at the doorway, where the break in the continuity of the curtain and its comparative shortness allowed it to be more easily raised, especially at the (lower) corners.

Within this limited but sufficiently capacious area, besides the principal object, the Tabernacle itself, there were only two others normally belonging to it, namely, the "Brazen Altar," and the "Laver."

The Altar of Burnt Offering

The former of these, often styled the Great Altar (in later litera-

---

12. Josephus, *Antiquities of the Jews,* III, vii, 2.

ture), or more appropriately the Altar of Burnt Offering, to distinguish it from the smaller Altar of Incense, was made strong and light for convenient transportation, thus superseding all former structures of the kind, but not exclusive of still larger earthen or stone altars, as in subsequent times (Exod. 20:24,25). The one under consideration was a hollow box[13] of acacia (shittim wood), five cubits square, and three cubits high (Exod. 27:1,8), cased all over its surface with sheets of copper (v. 2). It had a "horn" (i.e., an upright, tapering projection) at each corner, apparently formed by a triangular extension of the sides at their junction (v. 2). This was an ornamental and significant, rather than a strictly needful, appendage. An essential addition was the grate,[14] consisting of a copper network,[15] movable by a copper ring in each corner (v. 4), and

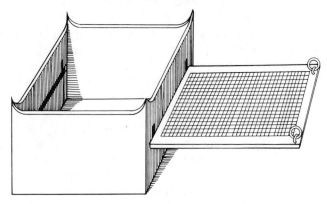

Fig. 3.—Altar of Burnt Offering, with the grate drawn out

13. "Hollow with boards" (27:8; 38:7), Hebrew *nebúb luchóth* (lit. "a hollow [*bored* through, like a tubular column, Jer. 52:21] of slabs [a different word from that used for the planks of the Tabernacle walls])." Their thickness was no doubt some definite proportion of a cubit, as we shall find all the dimensions about the structure to be (since, as Paine justly remarks, "A carpenter always works by his rule measure"); in this case probably one-eighth, or about $2\frac{1}{2}$ inches—not too great for so large a box, and one exposed to much hard service.

14. Hebrew *mikbár*, lit. "plaiting," used only of this contrivance; but a kindred term, *makbér*, is once applied to a coarse *cloth* (2 Kings 8:15).

15. Hebrew *résheth*, a term constantly applied to a net for catching animals.

placed below the top of the altar, halfway down the inside (v. 5). It thus appears that there was no cover to the altar at all, and probably no bottom, but only the grating, evidently for the fire, across it at the middle. This latter was supported by sliding through slits in the opposite sides of the altar, the rings projecting outside.[16] Through these rings were passed the copper-cased sidepoles used for carrying the whole on the march like a handbarrow (vv. 6, 7; comp. 38:5-7), while the grate was held fast by the ring and staves. The entire surface of the altar was therefore sheeted with copper inside and out, including the horns, so that the heat could not affect it; and the priests standing about it could conveniently manage the sacrificial fire, sliding the grate far enough out to take up the ashes that fell through it. The flame would be concentrated by being confined within the upper part of the altar box, and sufficient air to keep up a draught would enter by the crevices around the grate, especially those left to allow the rings to pass through or additional holes might be made for that purpose, if found to be necessary.

As the altar stood in the open court, and the fuel was above the center of the broad firebox, an ample supply of air would come in over the sides for ordinary purposes of combustion; and for the greater part of the day, and during the whole night, the fire was to be merely kept smoldering alive. On extraordinary occasions, the current would naturally be increased by excavating openings under the sides, and these could conveniently be closed by a stone at pleasure. A mound of earth might be raised on either side for

---

16. This is the arrangement of Paine in the last edition of his work, and entirely obviates the serious objections against all previous interpretations and conjectures. The Hebrew word rendered "compass" is *karkób,* an obscure one, and used only of this particular object, and designates the upper *margin* of the altar (which, as we shall see, was entirely different from that of the Altar of Incense). The word rendered "midst" is lit. *half,* as often elsewhere. Since the rings were *cast* (like those of all the other pieces that were similarly furnished—for this is expressly stated of all except the Incense altar [and the wallplanks], and "made" is there equivalent to "cast," as appears from a comparison in the other cases) and therefore solid, they must have been attached to the grate by means of staples *upon* its face (as the Hebrew invariably has it, in this as well as all the other cases).

ascending to the top whenever necessary. There was no occasion for steps or an inclined plane to reach it.

This altar was doubtless set directly upon the ground, and so might not inappropriately be called "an altar of earth" (Exod. 20:24). The gold-plated pieces of furniture indoor were probably placed upon fur rugs spread upon the ground. These skins were no doubt the same, or at least of the same character, as those that (as we shall eventually see) were used to cover up the sacred furniture on the march.

The utensils named (v. 3) in connection with the altar, all of copper, are "pans to receive [i.e., remove] the [greasy] ashes of the sacrifices,"[17] shovels for taking them up, basins for holding the blood of victims, with which the horns of the altar were smeared, fleshhooks for handling the roasting sacrifices, and managing the fire, and firepans for carrying coals for incense or other purposes.

From the fact (Num. 16:38,39) that similar vessels to these last, on one occasion (apparently not very long after the removal from Sinai) were readily used as additional plates for the Altar of Burnt Offering (probably on the edges of the firepot, where the wear would soonest tell), it would seem that these were simply square copper sheets folded at the corners (in gores like modern sheet-iron pans), and furnished with a plain handle (doubtless of the same, merely riveted on).

The Great Altar probably stood in the center of the open space of the court, about halfway between the entrance and the Tabernacle itself,[18] where it would be convenient of access to all worshipers, and leave room enough for the sacrifices. Upon it was maintained a perpetual fire of selected wood, except of course while on the march.

The Arabs who conduct travellers through the Desert of Sinai always keep up a fire during the night with the driftwood or brush which the winter rains bring down from the sides of the mountains. This is partly for company and partly for a sense of protection

---

17. Hebrew *dashshén,* a special word for these fatty ashes.

18. Exodus 40:29 is not determinative of the exact spot.

against surprise. The monkish local guides who escort tourists over the summit of Sinai are in the habit of touching a match to any dry shrub that they meet on the way; which seems a sort of reminiscence of the burning bramble that Moses saw. But the wild sage bushes, with which the plain and hillsides are dotted, are unmolested, although they stand quite dry, but still perfectly retaining their green color until the middle of March.

The Laver

Midway of this latter interval (Exod. 30:18), still in the medial line, stood the other conspicuous piece of apparatus for the service, namely, the Laver, which would be immediately at hand for the priests to bathe[19] before entering the Sanctuary, or approaching the Altar (vv. 19-21). It consisted of two parts, the Laver proper,[20] and its Foot[21] or pedestal. Neither the form nor the size is given.

Something, however, may be deduced from the etymology of the Hebrew term, and its use in other passages. It is derived from a root that seems primarily to mean *excavation by hammering,* and this would naturally yield a semi-globular hollow, which form is confirmed by the convenience for a lavatory, like a wash bowl or basin, and by the similar shape of the molten sea and the smaller lavers, which took its place in the Temple (1 Kings 7:30, 38, 40, 43; 2 Kings 16:17; 2 Chron. 4:6, 14), and which are denoted by the same word. It is elsewhere applied to a *chafing dish* for live coals (Zech. 12:6), and to a platform or *rostrum* (2 Chron. 6:13), which, although probably covered (as the other utensils seem not to have been), doubtless had the same urn-like form, and could not have been high, since no steps are spoken of in connection with it. In 1 Samuel 2:14, it is named first of four kinds of receptacles for boiling flesh, which seem to be enumerated in the order of their size, but could not have differed

---

19. Hebrew *racháts,* used of laving either the whole body, or any part.

20. Hebrew *kiyór,* a cooking *dish,* used generally of a pot, basin or pan.

21. Hebrew *ken,* lit. a "stand" or support, evidently an expansion of the shaft, probably with a turned-up rim so as to catch the drip from a faucet in the upper reservoir; for Orientals wash the hands by pouring water upon them from a ewer, and not by plunging them into a basin, which would defile the whole.

very much in their shape; namely, *kiyór* (prob. a *caldron,* A.V. "pan" here), *dud* (a large *pot* [lit. *boiler*], Job 41:20; Ps. 81:6; "kettle," here, "caldron," 2 Chron. 35:13; also a *"basket,"* 2 Kings 10:7; Jer. 24:2), *kalláchath* (from a word that seems to indicate *pouring;* a *kettle,* A.V. "caldron," here and in Mic. 3:3), and *parûr* (from a root significant of *hollowing by fracture,* a deep *pan,* as rendered in Num. 11:8; "pot" here and in Judg. 6:19).

Both parts (the Laver and the Foot) were obviously round, as the vessel was in fact merely a bowl with a base connected by a tapering neck, like a flat goblet. That it was shallow, and raised but little from the ground, may be inferred from its use, which was to wash the feet as well as the hands; and that it was comparatively small may be inferred from the fact that it was not intended for washing the entire person (vv. 19, 21). It was probably about two cubits in diameter and one and one half cubits high. Like all the utensils of the court, it was of copper, but in this case apparently somewhat alloyed; for it was a casting made of the metallic mirrors contributed by the female members of the congregation (38:8), such as the Egyptian ladies are known to have used.[22]

THE SANCTUARY

The Sanctuary or sacred fabric itself was situated at the front edge of the rear half of the entire enclosure, probably leaving equal spaces on either side and behind between its walls and those of the Court. It consisted of two portions, called, respectively, the Holy and the Most Holy places, the former occupying the forward room, and the latter one half the size in depth behind it (as will eventually appear). As both these were of the same width and general construction, we may most conveniently consider them together in point of architecture, and afterwards discuss their special features separately.

The Walls

The walls (which distinctively composed the *mishkán* or "Taber-

---

22. Wilkinson (*Ancient Egyptians,* 2, 345-7). These *specula* were of various metals, usually mixed, but not always nor properly bronze.

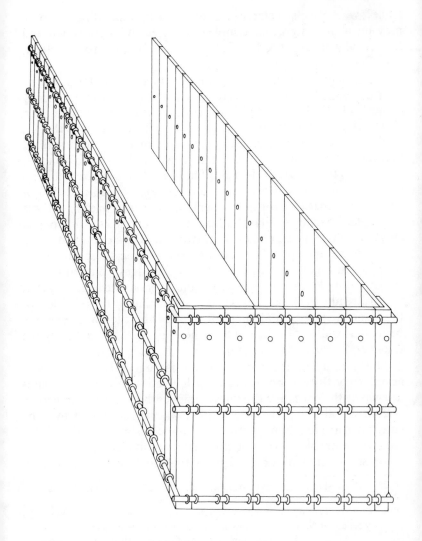

Fig. 4.—Wooden walls of the Tabernacle

nacle") were of a character, like all other parts of the edifice (if so we may term this migratory temple), to be easily taken down and re-erected whenever the divine signal should be given to that effect. (See Fig. 4.)

They essentially consisted of planks or "boards"[23] of the acacia or "shittim wood"[24] before mentioned, each ten cubits long, and $1\frac{1}{2}$ cubits wide (Exod. 26:16). Their entire surface was plated with sheets of gold. Twenty of these formed each sidewall (vv. 18, 20), held in a perpendicular position (v. 15) by means to be described presently, each plank having two tenons[25] in the foot to attach it securely to the ground as in a sill. The rear planks were eight in all (v. 25), of which six were like the foregoing (v. 22), and two of peculiar construction for the corners (v. 23). To form each of these last, a plank exactly similar to all the rest was divided throughout its length into two parts, one of them two-thirds of a cubit wide, and the other the remaining five-sixths of a cubit wide; these parts were then joined together at right angles by the edges, so as to form a "corner board," externally $\frac{5}{6}$ of a cubit on each side (one way that width already, the other $\frac{2}{3}$ plus $\frac{1}{6}$, because including the thickness of the associate plank), and internally $\frac{2}{3}$ of a cubit each way (one side being that width of itself, and the other $\frac{5}{6}$ minus $\frac{1}{6}$, as excluding the thickness of the attached plank).

This joining of the corner planks is suggested by Keil and adopted by Brown, but is yet of little avail with them, in consequence of the excessive thickness assigned by them to the planks themselves, although the latter writer makes the corner lap over the side. So near have some plans come to the correct solution of this part of the problem, without effectually accomplishing it.

These corner planks, being applied flush to the other rear planks,

---

23. Hebrew sing. *kéresh,* as being *hewn* out; used only of these planks and of the deck of a vessel ("benches," Ezek. 27:6). They were in fact almost logs, like floor timbers. The "boards" of 27:8 are a different word in the original, being that usually rendered "table," when this means merely a plate or slab.

24. The Arabic *seyál,* common in the Sinaitic desert, a thorny tree of moderate size, with firm and durable wood, closely resembling our yellow locust. The bark is smooth, and that of the limbs yellow, like the ailanthus. (See Fig. 39.)

25. Hebrew sing. *yad,* a "hand," as often elsewhere rendered. The analogy of

but extending around the corner over the rear edge and part of the width of the last side plank, completely fulfill the conditions of the case, and yield a satisfactory solution of several otherwise inexplicable problems.

1). The thickness of the planks themselves is proved, by the above calculation, to have been one-sixth of a cubit, which agrees with the statement (apparently from tradition or conjecture) of Josephus "four finger-breadths."[26]

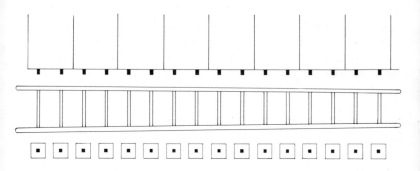

Fig. 5.—Comparison of the tenons and mortices of the wall planks with the rungs of a ladder

the other curtain posts leads us to conclude that they were of solid metal (therefore small) like that of the sockets, i.e., in the present case silver. These tenons are said to be "set in order," Hebrew *meshulláb*, a word that occurs nowhere else in Hebrew (except in *shaláb*, a "ledge," 1 Kings 7:28, 29), but in the cognate languages is applied to the *rungs* of a ladder, and seems to mean *regularly* occurring, i.e., at equal intervals (for this is the most essential feature of ladder rungs). We have arranged them, except those of the corner-plank, which are likewise two, but necessarily in a somewhat different position. In the parallel passage (Exod. 36:22) it is rendered "equally distant," and this is confirmed by a coincidence which can hardly be accidental. If these tenons (and the corresponding mortices) were equidistant, they would be $\frac{3}{4}$ of a cubit apart (from center to center) or about $15\frac{1}{2}$ inches, which actually is the most convenient and customary space between the rungs of a ladder. This correspondence to the natural type is illustrated by the annexed diagram. (See Fig. 5.) The tenons were probably square, in order to keep the sockets from revolving out of line, and of silver, so as to match the sockets.

26. Josephus, *Antiquities of the Jews,* III, vi, 3.

2). The requisite (interior) dimensions of the two apartments (Holy and Most Holy places) are secured. The proportional decimal character of all the measurements in the Court and its structures, and especially of the Sanctuary itself, and indeed the correspondence with these portions in the subsequent Temple (which were doubles of them, 1 Kings 6:2), point clearly to the conclusion that the width of the building (inside) was one-third its length. Thus the Most Holy place was exactly square, and the Holy place just twice as long as it was wide. The six full planks of the rear of the Holy of Holies ($6 \times 1\frac{1}{2} = 9$), added to that part of the split plank at each corner not taken up in covering the edge of the last side plank ($2 \times [\frac{2}{3} - \frac{1}{6} = \frac{1}{2}] = 1$), make exactly the ten cubits called for.

It is noteworthy that the dimensions of the Tabernacle itself are nowhere explicitly given, but are left to be inferred from a combina-

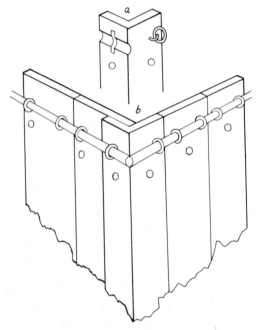

Fig. 6.—Corner plank of the Tabernacle (N. W. angle.)
a. Separate *b.* Combined

tion of the details. It is our opinion there would be uncertainty as to whether the internal or the external size were meant. Accordingly, measurements are definitely given with regard to the Court, the Ark, the Table, and the two Altars, because there could be no doubt on this point concerning them. This shows the minute carefulness of the sacred description. Moreover, in this way the corner joint is neatly closed, which would otherwise show on the side, instead of the end of the rectangle, as usual with joiners; and the whole angle would also be greatly strengthened as well as ornamented by the overlapping on the longer side.

3). This clears up the obscure phraseology employed (v. 24) concerning these corner planks, "And they shall be coupled together beneath, and they shall be coupled together above the head of it unto one ring [lit. and together they shall become whole upon the compound plank's head toward the one (or first) ring]." This plainly means that the two half-planks were to be joined together from bottom to top, and were likewise fastened by the same end-most ring (namely, that of the rear side-plank). By inspecting the annexed diagram (Fig. 7), it will be seen how exactly true this last

Fig. 7.—Socket of the Tabernacle
a. Top *b.* Edge

peculiarity was; for the first barring of the side planks at the corner must have passed entirely through the overlap of the rear plank, and the ring (when the bar was passed through it) would hold the corner firmly together. This was a very important fact (especially at the top) in a structure destitute of a framework.

In the adjustment which we have adopted it will be seen that the planks are held together laterally (so as not to be parted by the strain of the end stays) by the roof canvas, which is buttoned down close on the knobs all around the three sides (and across the front likewise). At the rear corners which are held together by this arrangement of the corner planks, this security is unnecessary, and therefore (on account of the slit or notch in the selvedge at that point, as we shall eventually see) it is there dispensed with.

In order to receive the tenons in the ends of the planks, sockets of solid silver were laid upon the ground (corresponding to those of copper for the Court), two for each plank (Exod. 26:19). As each socket weighed one talent (38:27), T. O. Paine has ingeniously calculated their size as being half a cubit square, and one-sixth of a cubit thick.

We arrive at the same result by a different calculation. Each socket, if solid, would contain $\frac{1}{24}$ of a cubic cubit ($\frac{1}{2} \times \frac{1}{2} \times \frac{1}{6}$), or 365.6 cubic inches ($\frac{1}{24} \times [20.625 = 20\frac{5}{8}]^3$). But from this must be deducted the mortice ($[\frac{1}{16} \times \frac{1}{16} \times \frac{1}{6}] \times [20\frac{5}{8}]^3$), or 5.6 cubic inches, leaving exactly 360 cubic inches of silver for the socket. Now, as a cubic inch of silver weighs 2,652.8 grains [one grain weighs 0.0648 grams] (at 62° F.), the socket would weigh 955,008 grains. Again, as there are 3,000 shekels in a talent, and a shekel weighed about 280 grains (original standard), the talent or socket would weigh about 840,000 grains; which sufficiently agrees with the former product, especially as some alloy (0.138 parts of copper) was probably added to harden the metal. We note that the estimate of 280 grains to the shekel is exactly that of the Assyrian standard.[27] This subject has been greatly confused by writers not observing that the shekel was eventually a *coin* as well as a weight, and that its value, therefore, greatly varied in the different metals (gold, silver, and copper) used for money, as well as in different periods. The ancient specimens that exist have also been worn by circulation. The earliest Jewish shekels extant are of the age of the Maccabees, and were struck on the debased Phoenician standard of 220 grains to the silver shekel, equivalent to the Greek *tetradrachm,* which was itself originally much higher, and was lowered in the Ptolemaic period to 260 grains.

The ancient native Egyptian metrology was related to the Hebrew in measures but not in weights. The silver shekels of Maccabaean date in the British Museum at London, as we have ascertained by personal inquiry, weigh severally 220, 216.5, 215, 213.2 and 213 grains, according to the degree of wear. There is also a half

27. Madden, F.W., *Jewish Coinage,* p.264, note.

shekel of the same metal and age, which weighs only 99.1 grains, being very much worn. Copper shekels usually very greatly exceed these specimens in weight. Most or all of the silver shekels sold to travellers in Palestine are imitations, and genuine copper shekels are exceedingly rare. A copper (really bronze) double stater (so to call it) or tetradrachm (adopted as an equivalent in weight for a quadruple shekel) of the period of the Ptolemies (the obverse has only the Ptolemaic conventional head of Alexander the Great as Jupiter Ammon, and the reverse the title "of Ptolemy king," with an eagle grasping thunderbolts, and the indeterminate mint-mark *delta* between its legs), obtained by the author from the natives at Gaza (where it may possibly have been struck), weighs 1051 grains, although considerably worn; which yields about 263 grains to the shekel. The gold and silver coins of the Ptolemies gradually decline in the successive reigns from 265 to 174 grains to the drachm or shekel.[28] The Greek coinage of the Seleucidae, during the same period, exhibits a similar deterioration from 265 to 200 grains.[29] The copper currency of course was less subject to the temptation to fall off from the standard, which thus appears to have stood, at the Macedonian conquest, at not less than 265 grains to the shekel. We cannot, therefore, safely fix it lower than 280 grains to the shekel for the time of Moses.

Presuming that the mortice-holes (probably one-sixteenth cubit, or about $1\frac{1}{4}$ inch, square) were in the middle of the sockets, and the (center of the) tenons three-eighths of a cubit from the edge of the plank, the sockets would leave a space between them of one-fourth of a cubit, except those of the corner planks, which, if like all the rest they were two to each (as the total demands, 96 in all, Exod. 26:19, 21, 25; besides one under each of the four columns that supported the veil, v. 32; 38:27), would nicely fit in between those of the adjoining planks, as in the annexed diagram.

Our arrangement is the only one hitherto proposed that makes

---

28. Poole, R.T., *Catalogue of Egyptian Coins in the British Museum,* pp. 1-120.

29. Poole, R.T., *Catalogue of Syrian Coins in the British Museum,* pp. 1-112.

all the sockets of the same size and proper form and in their places without interference with one another. Lack of uniformity would have caused great confusion and delay.

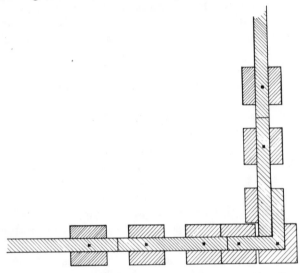

Fig. 8.—Arrangement of the corner sockets (S.W. angle)

For the purpose of keeping the planks in line, three series of bars were provided, made of acacia wood overlaid with gold, to pass through rings of gold stapled into the face of the planks outside (Exod. 26:26-29). There were five bars (in three rows) for each bent, the middle one continuous for the whole stretch,[30] and the upper

---

30. The last clause should be rendered, "Five bars for the planks of the side of the Tabernacle, [namely] for the two flanks [i.e., ends of the rear] westward" (Exod. 26:27). These bars, of course, were round, as they were passed through *rings* (Hebrew sing. *tabáath*, something *impressed*, hence a finger or *seal* ring; the same word used of all the other circular rings of the Tabernacle furniture). A plausible mode of arranging them is to make them in five rows, the middle or third one passing through the center of the planks themselves; but there are insuperable objections to this: (1). It disagrees with the text, for this bar would not then pass through rings at all (v. 29, "rings [of] gold [for] places [lit., "houses"] for the bars"); and it would no more "reach from end to end" than all the others. (2).

and lower ones divided into two lengths (of course, in the middle, and probably dowelled with a pin in the adjoining ends).[31] The diameter of the bars and rings not being given (nor indeed the size of any of the bars and rings of the edifice and furniture), we may suppose these to have been stout sticks (probably one-fourth of a cubit in diameter),[32] as two of them were very long, and all were exposed to a severe strain. The upper and lower courses were probably set as near as possible to the extremities of the planks, i.e., as we shall see, about the middle of the last cubit. From the above noticed mention of a "first ring" in the case of the corner plank, we infer that each had two of these rings.

You will note that the text distinctly constructs the two corner planks out of two of the rear planks only, not each of them out of a rear plank and a side plank combined. It also speaks of but one set of rings in this connection, namely, those intended for the bars. Again, it will be perceived that the rear has sixteen sockets assigned to it, and each side forty; therefore, the overlap of the corner plank has no extra socket, and it needs none, for it rests on the last side socket.

The whole structure was doubtless braced with cords and tent pins, which would be conveniently fastened to the copper knobs[33] in

---

Unless the planks were made inordinately thick, this bar (evidently of the same size and material as the rest) would have to be made so slender that it would break with its own weight; and in any case it would be impossible to push it through so long an aperture.

31. So Josephus understands the case (*Antiquities* III, vi, 3), for he occasionally has a good suggestion, although he makes a sad bungle of most of the description.

32. If the bars are thus made of the same size as the pillars and tent poles, they will exactly continue the slope of the roof canvas over the eaves at the same angle as the peak. They will be partly buried in the side wrap of the corner planks, but enough of the latter will remain not cut away for the requisite strength, on account of the necessary projection of the staples for the rings.

33. Hebrew sing. *kéres* (erroneously rendered A.V. "tache," i.e., hook), which Paine ingeniously compares with its kindred *karsól*, the ankle, from the striking resemblance to the latter as viewed from behind. See the remarks on these fixtures farther on.

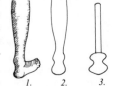

Fig. 9.—Tache and ankle compared
1. Natural form *2.* Typical form
3. Artificial form

the planks, set in the outer face one cubit (as we will hereafter see) below the eaves, as a point of attachment likewise for the roof curtain (vv. 11, 13), to be presently considered. These tent pins, like those of the court posts, were no doubt of copper. We presume shorter stays of the same kind were attached to the gold knobs on the inside, as the roof canvas would not be a sufficient support.

The only other attachment to the planks was a double blanket[34] of peltry on the outside, doubtless suspended on the curtain knobs, and evidently intended to cover the joints, and thus keep out the wind and rain, like a shingled weather-boarding, or the tarpaper sheathing of modern houses (v. 14 and parallels). It consisted of a sheet of fur from some kind of animal,[35] doubtless with the hair side inward next to the gold face of the planks, and another of ram-skin, dyed red, over it, with the hair side out, so as to shed the rain from the eaves.[36] Their dimensions are not given because, the skins being of indeterminate size, so many of them as were found necessary were to be stitched together for the purpose. They, of course, extended to the top of the planks, slits (like buttonholes) being made in them (as their toughness would allow) for the reception of the knobs on which they hung.

The Roof

As to the roof, the first question that necessarily arises is, Did the edifice have a peak or was it flat-roofed? This is definitely settled by

34. Hebrew *makséh,* a *covering,* applied only to this particular thing and to a precisely similar service (as we shall see) in Noah's ark (Gen. 8:13), although the root from which it is derived frequently occurs of clothing or other envelopes, especially for the sake of concealment. It was a perpendicular sheeting.

35. Hebrew *táchash,* (A.V. "badger," R.V. "seal"), usually thought to be some marine creature, but possibly the Angora goat, noted for its fine long silky fleece. (See p. 122, note.)

36. In all the passages where these are mentioned the Hebrew term *millemálah* (lit. "from as to upward"), which has unfortunately been rendered simply "above," but means *from the top downward* (like the water of the Flood, Gen. 7:20, which was fifteen cubits deep from the surface to the summits of the submerged mountains), stands at the end of the clause in the original, and applies to both sheets of skin. The position assigned them by all writers previous to Paine, namely, *on the roof,* is too absurd to be entertained for a moment.

the single word *tent*,[37] which is distinctively applied to the upper portion of the structure, erected "upon" the Tabernacle walls (40:19), and which by no possibility of usage, in any language, can mean anything but a canvas covering with a peak. The necessity of shedding rain, and the invariable style of Bedouin encampments, moreover fix this as an incontrovertible principle of architecture in such cases. An Oriental house roof of mortar, clay, etc., is entirely another affair, not to be thought of here.

Nearly all the proposed plans of the Tabernacle, being on the flat roof principle, fail to make any adequate provision for securing either set of curtains, or indeed for disposing of them at all. Even Ferguson, although, as a professional architect, he perceives the necessity of a peak roof, is obliged to extend the roof sheets into unwarranted wing slopes, and to furl the others in rolls at the gables, where they would soon mildew and decay. The misery of all these devices is that they bring the previous Veil in the worst possible place, namely, directly under the gap in the roof occasioned by the union of the curtains by means of loops and S or C hooks. To pile the *"tachash"* and ram skins on the top, in order *to stop the leak,* is a pitiful contrivance. The "taches," the true meaning of which Paine was the first to point out, are the key to the whole situation, as they afford a firm support to all the connections. The Revised Version renders them "clasps" at a venture (or from *Josephus*). These would be unsuitable for loops, and do not mend the

---

37. Hebrew *óhel,* constantly used of a canvas tent; but unfortunately rendered "covering" in the A.V. in this case (Exod. 26:7, etc.). We might securely rest upon this ground of evidence, were it the only one. Those who have any doubt of its sufficiency will find it impregnably fortified by the subsequent adjustments, especially the width and arrangement of the roof curtains. A flat roof would have become moldy and rotten irretrievably the first month of winter, especially with the fur robes piled on the top. Moreover, how unsightly would have been a mere box, like a coffin with a pall over it! A flat canvas roof, however tightly stretched, must have sagged so as to catch tons of water, if impervious; breaking the canvas, and indeed causing the whole structure to collapse. Or if, as is more probable, the rain would penetrate the canvas bowl, it would deluge the apartments, especially the Most Holy place, where no one was allowed to enter, even for the purpose of lifting the roof with a rod, in order to allow the water to run off. In every point of view, the flat roof scheme is utterly impractical.

matter. The rainfall during the showers in the winter on the Sinaitic peninsula is often prodigious, and snow occasionally falls to the depth of several inches in the valleys about Mt. Sinai. In March, 1874, the author, with his party, was overtaken by a snow storm at Mt. Sinai, of such severity as to compel them to take refuge in the convent there for several days. Writers who think only of the dry season have little knowledge in the case.

Accordingly, we have an account of the roofing material, which is goat's hair canvas, exactly such as is employed for Arab tents today, being generally of a foxy black or brownish hue (Song of Sol. 1:5). It was woven in eleven pieces, each thirty cubits long and

Fig. 10.—Arab tents in the south of Judah
It will be perceived, from the white stripes on one of these tents, that the cloth runs *horizontally*.

four wide (26:7, 8), and these widths were joined[38] into two large separate sheets, one containing five and the other six of the pieces of cloth (v. 9). The extra or sixth "curtain" or width of the second sheet was employed for a peculiar purpose, namely, not as a part of the roof covering, but to be wrapped across the front and rear gables.[39] In order to do this it must have been attached to its fellow-widths not by the selvedge, like the others, but *at the end* of the narrowest.

---

38. Hebrew *chabár*, to *associate* together as companions, (A.V. "couple,") evidently by sewing into a sheet (v. 10, where a derivative of the same verb is used); so also of the side curtains (v. 3). The same verb indeed is used to denote the junction of the two sheets on the knobs (vv. 6, 11), because they are there also united by the edges, although in a different manner. If the intention had been simply to join the two sections of each set of curtains into one immense sheet, they would, of course, have been sewed together at once, like the individual widths, instead of resorting to the clumsy and imperfect seam done by means of loops and hooks, as interpreters have done.

39. That this is the true meaning of the expression in Exod. 26:9, "And shalt double [Hebrew *kaphál*, to "fold," without regard to the number of thicknesses; for it is used of repetition indefinitely] the sixth curtain in the forefront [lit.

Paine was the first writer, from Josephus down, to suggest an endwise union of either set of Tabernacle curtains; but he joins this sixth roof curtain wholly at the end of its fellow, folding all of it across the rear of the building, for which it is more than enough, although he makes the Tabernacle twelve cubits wide by $29\frac{1}{2}$ long (inside measurement), or $12\frac{1}{3}$ wide by thirty long (outside)—both disproportionate numbers.

We have, therefore, two goat's-hair sheets, each thirty cubits long by twenty wide, but one of them with extensions (or "L parts" so to

---

"towards the front of the face"] of the Tent [not "Tabernacle," as in the A.V.; for there was no wooden wall, or Tabernacle part, in the front of the building]," is clear from the use of the same phrase to describe the position of the engraved plate on the high priest's headdress (Exod. 28:37), "upon the forefront," certainly not across the back of his head. In v. 12, accordingly, the expression is very different, "[As to] the remnant [lit. "overflow," i.e., extended flap] that remaineth [lit. "the superfluous," i.e., jutting out on this end] of [lit. "in"] the curtains of the Tent [i.e., roof part], half of the [not "the half," as in the A.V.] curtain that remaineth [lit. as before, "the superfluous," i.e., jutting out portion on the end] shall [or "thou shalt"] hang [lit. cause to "overflow"] over [lit. "upon"] the backside of the Tabernacle [i.e., wall part]." Nor is either of these two parts of the surplus or sixth roof curtain the same with that part immediately afterwards described (v. 13), "And a [rather "the"] cubit on the one side [lit. "from this"], and a [lit. "the"] cubit on that side [lit. "from that"], of that which remaineth [lit. "in the superfluous," i.e., excess] in the length [not parallel with the eaves, but across them] of the curtains of the Tent [i.e., roof part], it [omit this word as ungrammatical, not found in the text, and misleading] shall hang [lit. "be overflowing"] over [lit. "upon"] the sides of the Tabernacle [i.e., wall part], on this side [lit. "from this"] and on that side [lit. "from that"] to cover it." Mark that in v. 9 only so much of the sixth curtain is to project at that end as is necesasry to fold (once) across the *front* (i.e., ten cubits); while in v. 12 half (ten cubits) of the residue (twenty cubits) of the curtain projecting at the other end is to be folded (twice, but separately reckoned, as we shall see) across the *rear;* and still again, in v. 13, there is a (different) excess of one cubit to be folded down *each side.* This last "length of the curtains of the tent" is not reckoned horizontally, but vertically, as "breadth" is in 38:18; in both cases *height* being really meant.

Note that the preposition here employed is *'el* (A.V., "in"), which means a flexure in a *horizontal* direction; not *'al,* which would have indicated *vertical* motion. With this agrees the other distinctive term here added, namely, *mûl,* which is lit. *cut off,* i.e., an abrupt and perpendicular surface. The extra roof curtain, therefore, was neither spread nor furled overhead, or on either side, but was used to enclose the upright gables in front and rear.

speak), one twice as long as the other, in the manner of the diagram. (See Fig. 11.)

Again, as these elongations of one of the widths were to be folded across the gables, the other widths must likewise run horizontally, but along and upon the roof. For this purpose they would be exactly long enough (for the twenty planks, each $1\frac{1}{2}$ cubits wide, make also thirty cubits), and their combined width (twenty cubits) would likewise be exactly wide enough to go over the ridge, and buckle down over the knobs in the planks. If the peak be an isosceles triangle of 70° (a sacred number) at the apex (giving $55\frac{1}{2}$° at each of the other vertices, a very proper slope for a roof), the base being $10\frac{1}{2}$ cubits (i.e., the width of the room, plus the thickness of the walls), each side of the roof will be exactly nine cubits wide, and these with the cubit below each eave will make up the required sum. This fact is very important, for there was no other provision, unless possibly a pin at each end of the middle bar, to prevent the tops of

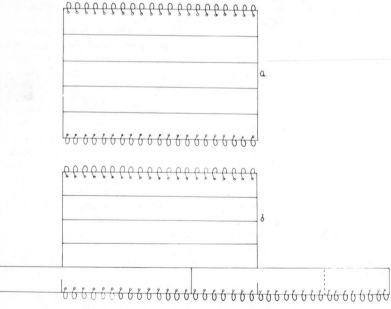

Fig. 11.—Roof curtains as made up and furnished with loops
a. Five widths *b.* Six widths

the planks from parting laterally (as the strain of the transverse stay cords at the ends of the line would certainly make them do), except the stretching of this roof canvas across their face. Moreover, this roof canvas, stretched tight across the ridge would keep the whole of the building from parting, under the outward strain of the stay cords directly opposite.

The sixth or surplus width of the larger roof curtain, as we have seen, was folded across the bottom part of each gable, partly closing this triangle, and preventing the draft of air through the rooms (which were otherwise entirely open in the front peak). (The reader should note how important a purpose the extra roof sheet also served in covering the otherwise exposed top of the rear planks and their attachments. Uniformity in this respect is maintained all around the three sides of the edifice.) As it was thirty cubits long (like all of its fellows), one third of it was sufficient to do this, single-fold.[40] This gives us a clue to the peculiar significance of the word translated "double" in Exodus 26:9.[41] It suggests that the

---

40. The peak, if an angle of 70°, as we have assumed, would be very nearly $7\frac{1}{2}$ cubits perpendicular height above the tops of the planks, and the gable curtain would rise three cubits high above them, so as nearly to fill up the rest of the triangle, in the manner shown by the diagram (Fig. 12). The opening at the peak

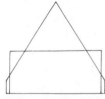

was needed for light and ventilation, serving both as a window and a chimney; but a full current of air would have put out the lights of the candelabrum. The gores at the top of the folds (occasioned by the slant of the roof) would be tucked in between the two layers of roof canvas. The small gores at the corners of the eaves (occasioned by the extra width of the planks beyond the peak) may be covered by extending the skin blankets a little above the tops of the planks, where they would likewise be held between the layers of the roof canvas. (See Fig. 13.) In the same manner they probably lapped around the front edges, so as to be buttoned

Fig. 12.—Rear gable nearly closed by the sixth roof curtain. The front bagle was partly closed in like manner, but by a single fold.

to the hooks in the endposts of the doorway. If any further support were needed for the front fold of canvas, it might also be buttoned to an extra hook in the central post. It should be observed that these immaterial points are left to the discretion of the builders.

41. Hebrew *kaphál* (noted above), which properly means to "*wrap* around," but is frequently used in the sense of *duplication,* and sometimes in that of continued *reiteration.*

curtain in question was actually laid on "*double* thickness". In other words, that the other part of it was employed in repeating the same process, simply by reversing the operation of folding. This additional security against the weather was doubtless extended to the other roof curtains, and that will effectively, readily and consistently dispose of the remaining or smaller sheet of five widths. The whole roof, in short, was of double canvas, like the "fly" over the best modern tents.

The lower edge of each sheet was buttoned securely over the curtain knobs by means of loops[42] (doubtless likewise of goat's hair, probably twisted into cord) attached to the selvedge (v. 10).

The language used here is peculiar. "Thou shalt make fifty loops on the edge [lit. "lip"] of the one [rather "first"] curtain [i.e., width], that is outmost [lit. "extreme"] in the coupling [i.e., sheet, as sewed together], and fifty loops in the edge of the curtain that coupleth the second [rather, "(namely,) the second coupling"]." This cannot mean merely, as understood by most interpreters, that each sewed sheet had fifty loops on one of its edges; for besides the circumlocution to express so simple an idea, they would then be exactly alike in this respect, whereas the phraseology expresses considerable differences between them. With Paine, we take the statement to signify that each sheet, *as applied to the building,* covered the space occupied by that number of loops, reckoning the whole circuit of the roof, from one front corner round the sides and back, to the opposite front corner. In other words, the fifty loops of each sheet include the rear, as being necessary in order to complete their circuit. Inasmuch as this was double, the inner fold is attributed to the elongated inner sheet, of which it was actually a part, and the outer fold to the outer sheet, of which it was the complement. This mode of estimation is favored by the reference, in the passage itself, to the extremities of the line of measurement. The uniformity of proportion was thus maintained, although the sheets

---

42. Hebrew only in the plural *lulaóth* (lit. "windings"), *nooses,* used solely of this particular thing, and a kindred word *lulím,* a spiral staircase (1 Kings 6:8). These loops were probably threaded through eyelets in the edges of the curtains; those of the roof canvas apparently having the ends merely tied together in a ring, and those of the side drapery knotted at the back. (Compare Fig. 16.)

themselves were unequal, and their attachments varied accordingly.

For the sake of convenient comparison we place here, in parallel columns, an exact translation of this and the remarkably similar, yet characteristically different, account of the other set of hangings for the same structure (vv. 4, 5), which we will presently consider in detail. The words in the parallel account (Exod. 36:8-18) are identical (in the original) except as to tense.

Roof curtains (Exodus 26:10)

And thou shalt make fifty loops upon the lip (edge) of the first curtain [as] the endmost in the joining, and fifty loops upon the lip (edge) of the curtain [as] the second joining.

Side curtains (Exodus 26:4, 5)

And thou shalt make loops of violet on the lip (edge) of the first curtain from an end in the joining, and so shalt thou make in the lip (edge) of the curtain [as] in the endmost in the second joint. Fifty loops shalt thou make in the first curtain, and fifty loops shalt thou make in the end of the curtain which [is] in the second joint; the loops receptive one toward the other.

The two Hebrew terms carefully used in the above passages for distinguishing the two kinds of margin which every piece or sheet of cloth necessarily has, must not be confounded, as they seem to be by every interpreter whom we have consulted, namely, *sapháh* (lit. *lip*, A.V. "edge"), which is the *selvedge* or lateral (woven) margin; and *katséh* (lit. *end*, A.V. "edge"), or its equivalent *katsáh* (lit. *end*, A.V. "selvedge"), with its derivative *kitsyón* (lit. *endwise*, or *endmost*, A.V. "uttermost," "utmost"), which denotes the *raw edge* or terminal (cut) margin. The *lip* is the natural border of the mouth (which is not a *gash* in the face), while the other term (from *katsáh*, to *clip* off) is the abrupt *end*.

It is to be borne in mind that the rear laps of the roof curtains, although exactly one third the length of those on the side of the building, each require 8 loops, instead of 7, in order to meet the corresponding knobs, which are closer together at the corner than elsewhere. (See Fig. 11.)

The fact that each sheet had fifty of these loops, while there were but fifty of the knobs in all to which they were attached (v. 11), confirms our position that the curtains were double, one being fastened on directly over the other. If all these fifty loops had been sewed on a single edge of thirty cubits' length, they would not only have been greatly crowded (occurring about half-a-cubit apart), but would also have been out of harmony with all the other associated spaces. The cubit in the span of the canvas across the roof was carried down over the eaves, and served to close the joint perfectly, shedding the drip to the ramskins (v. 12).

This "superfluity" or overlap (different from that of v. 12) is said to be "in the length of the curtains," because it showed vertically when hung. (Comp. the converse expression in 38:18.) The length of the exterior or roof curtains is given according to the *inside* dimensions of the building, as we shall see is done with great exactness also in the case of the interior or wall curtains. But as the outside of the building was, of course, larger than its inside (by the thickness of the walls), the extra length of roof canvas falls short considerably (namely, $\frac{2}{6}$ [at the front] + $\frac{8}{6}$ [at the rear, where the corner board is doubled] = $1\frac{2}{3}$ cubits in all) in wrapping across the gable three times. To meet this deficiency we must suppose that a notch or slit (the raw end, of course, bound or hemmed to prevent ravelling) was made in the edge of this extension at the corner, running up sufficiently to meet the slope of the roof (i.e., about $\frac{1}{2}$ cubits).

This break in the continuity of the looped edge facilitates the attribution of the loops of the dissevered selvedges to the under and the outer layers of the roof canvas. This is required in order to maintain uniformity in the number of the loops; especially as the layers were put on separately, with the skin blankets between them. Should we ask, Why was not this sixth roof curtain made a little longer at once, in order to cover the corners completely? We reply that this would not only have upset the uniformity of dimensions (a point which we will see is important in the symbolism—where no odd fractions are permitted), but would also have caused a larger and thicker gore at the corner than could have been neatly tucked in between the layers of the roof canvas, especially as the extension must then have been made at least two cubits longer, to wrap (four times) over the bars and rings of the corner. All this surplus would be accumulated in the gore. The triangular gap at the corner may be covered by carrying up the blanket of skins sufficiently above the tops of the planks. The fulness thus occasioned in their short gore may be relieved by a slit of their fold likewise at that point (which could not be done in the longer fold of the roof canvas without dissevering it entirely). (See Fig. 13.) The ridge remains precisely

Fig. 13.—Fold in the roof curtain at the corner
The cut exhibits the outer layer of the canvas at the northwest angle. The little gore at the left-hand top of the rear wrap is brought out of the tuck under the side (or roof) curtain's edge, so as to show it. The inner layer goes under this, coinciding with it, and the double blanket of skins between them.

thirty cubits long, and this regulates the length of the roof canvas. The ends of the roof sheets, it will be observed, are maintained square, and the tent poles perfectly plumb, while the rear gable is a little wider at the bottom, so as to cover the tops of the planks. An extra hook or two may be inserted in the tent pole to support the upper edge of this front and rear lap, and one also in the edge of each front plank, if necessary; for the number of hooks (and of their corresponding eyelets) is nowhere stated.

Paine, to whom we are indebted for this segregation of the eleventh roof curtain and its loops, is unable to use it to advantage because he makes the building twelve cubits wide instead of ten. He has, therefore, not enough material to wrap across the front gable, but too much to wrap twice across the rear gable. The six surplus cubits of curtain must therefore, on his scheme, be folded away between the side layers, and go unfurnished with loops, although they occur in the very middle of the looped portion, without anything to mark the break in the continuity of the loops.

The roof was obviously sustained by an extension upward of the central doorpost (soon to be considered) in front of the entire building, and no doubt by a similar one in the rear, with probably a third in the middle of the whole edifice. These served as tent poles, and their heads were probably bevelled on a curve so as not to perforate the canvas. They were, of course, stayed by extra ropes near the top, doubtless by means of a noose, kept from slipping down (as in the court posts) by an additional hook, which last would likewise serve to receive an eyelet in the edge of the roof canvas at the peak. There is no evidence, as there was no need, of any other posts or crossropes (or crosspoles, nor of a ridgepole (or ridgerope), which is not customary in Arab tents. A ridgepole would have been excessively heavy if stout enough to prevent any sag, and a ridgerope would have been no stronger than the canvas itself. Arab tents have ordinarily nine perpendicular poles, arranged in three rows, of three each, which correspond respectively to the ridge and the two eaves. The roof canvas is merely thrown over their tops, extending in a long slope on all the four sides to the ground, to which it is stretched tight by cords and pins. The entrance is simply by raising a flap of this canvas, which in the daytime and fine weather is kept open by an extra pole or two standing obliquely outward like an awning. The interior is divided into two apartments (the front usually for the men, and the rear for the women) by a screen stretched along the middle line of poles. All this is exactly analogous to the arrangement of the Tabernacle, except that the walls supply the place of the side rows of poles, and that the partition is thrown further back.

The central tent pole among the Bedouin is the general receptacle of loose utensils, which are hung upon it, as was the practice among the ancient Assyrians.[43] It would be a most convenient place for suspending the sacerdotal wardrobe, when not in use (Lev. 16:23).

Fig. 14.—Probable form of the first and third "Tabernacles" (See pp. 11 and 13)
The Veil is seen across the middle of the tent, corresponding to the partition between the men's and the women's apartments.

Occasionally, especially on the outskirts of civilization, we meet with an Oriental tent that has an *octagonal* form, with one central post, and the others disposed circularly around it, the outer walls falling perpendicularly from them to the ground, and braced by the usual cords and pins. This strikingly approaches the plan of the Tabernacle, and we have suggested that the tents, temporarily erected for sacred purposes by Moses and David, may have been of this description. (See Fig. 14.) One such is exhibited in the photograph from which Fig. 10 is copied, and another with a wing curtain also. This form has the advantage of greater compactness of space for the headroom afforded, and may serve to distinguish the residence of a noted personage.

43. Layard, A.H., *Nineveh,* ii, 214.

The Interior Hangings

The interior hangings of the building were of a far finer texture than the roof curtains.

The entrance was closed by a *screen* precisely like that of the outer Court (Exod. 26:36), supported by five pillars in exactly the same manner, except that they were overlaid entirely with gold (hence requiring no separate caps), and that the hooks were of gold (v. 37), the sockets (and, of course, the tenons) being of copper. We presume that these pillars were of the same form and size also, both with each other and with those of the Court, and we have already supposed the central one to be carried up to the height required to support the peak.

Placing the first and the fifth pillar as close to the walls as the side curtain will allow,[44] we have four openings left of about two cubits each (or $3\frac{1}{2}$ feet) in the clear, which is ample for a person to pass through. The pillars, of course, were stayed fore and aft by cords and pins, but needed no bracing laterally, as the rods held the tops equidistant, and the side walls kept the whole line from falling either way.

The *wall drapery,* already several times referred to, consisted of ten pieces of cloth woven of the same materials as the doorway screens, but in this case only four cubits wide, and twenty-eight long; sewed together into two large sheets, and buttoned with loops (of violet [cord])[45] to golden knobs in the walls, altogether analo-

---

44. The two copper sockets for these pillars (or posts) may be set adjoining the silver sockets of the planks, with a small interval between as a mortice to receive the copper tenon. The rear tent pole will exactly fall between two silver sockets, and its copper socket may be sunk below them out of sight.

45. In the case of the roof curtains, the material of the loops was not specified, because it would be taken for granted as being the same with the simple material of the curtains themselves. But in the present case there is need of stating which of the two materials, linen and wool, that composed the side curtains, was selected, and, again, which of the three colors used in dyeing it was chosen. As they were made of twisted two-stranded cord, and this again of either single or double thread, the three colors could not have been employed in equal proportions in their composition, nor would such a mottled color have been suitable in itself or consonant with the other colored objects. Of the three the cerulean was far the

gous to the roof curtains (26:1-6; 36:8-13). (See the comparison of the language used respecting these two series of curtains, as given above and below.) These two sheets are explicitly said to be exactly alike, and to be similarly furnished with loops; hence, borrowing the hint from the duplication of the roof canvas, we presume they were intended to be hung *double* along the walls. This suggestion is countenanced by the special Hebrew word employed to denote their combination, *makbil* (26:5; 36:12, only; A.V. "held," "take hold"), lit. "causing to receive," being the participle of a causative conjugation of the verb *kabál,* usually rendered "to receive." The reader should note that the loops "take hold one of another" (as the A.V. in 26:5), not "held one curtain to another" (as the A.V. in 36:12). They fall directly upon each other, being duplicated like the curtains themselves. If they were hung double, they were sewed together *endwise,* like the fifth and sixth cloths of the larger roof sheet. This last-named fact is the final justification of the singular phraseology (as previously exhibited) designating the resemblances as well as the differences between the two sets of curtains. They alike had fifty selvedge loops in the entire course of each layer as put on the building. The "coupling" or combination, meant in this connection not being that of sewing together into one sheet (as in 26:3, 9; 36:10, 18), but that of bringing the corresponding sheets over each other in the erection (as in 26:6; 36:13). Hence the use of the term "endmost" curtain (i.e., the piece sewed *at the end* of its neighbor, and not at the side or selvedge, like the rest) only in speaking of the *first* sheet of the roof covering; whereas it (or its

---

most appropriate on the overlaid background ("blue and gold"). But there was another and more imperative reason for the use of "blue" (violet) as the color of these loops. They were always attached, as we shall eventually see, to or near the upper corners of the violet stripe in the cloth, the eyelets, through which they were woven, being set entirely within that color. The only exception to this rule (so obviously proper; for violet loops on a different colored edge would have been unseemly, when in plain sight) is in the extreme corners, where there is no violet stripe to be shown, and where the union is concealed by the two folds coming together, as do the ends of the loops also. The stripes of different colors, woven, are maintained of uniform width and succession in the same piece of cloth, as must have been done in weaving them. (See Fig. 16.)

equivalent "end") is applied to both side sheets. The terms "first" and "second" here, as applied to the "curtains" or the "couplings," mean not those previously described as five-width or six-width sheets (with regards to the roof canvas the smaller one is named first, whereas here it is the larger that is thus designated), but those *laid on* first or second, i.e., the under and the outer layer respectively.

We note, in order to exemplify the exact characteristic of this whole text (although at first sight almost unintelligible), that the description of the side curtains is repeated (with some intentional variation) in both accounts, although their arrangement was really very simple. That of the roof curtains, however, which were more complicated, both in themselves, and especially in the numeration of the loops, is but once given in each account. The reason for this lies not merely in the circumstance that the former are mentioned earlier in the sacred narrative, and therefore more fully and explicitly, while the latter, coming in immediately afterwards, are given more briefly and vaguely, as if but a repetition of the other in all subordinate points not clearly specified. It is also because definiteness of meaning requires it. In the case of the side curtains, we have at large the color of the loops and their selvedge position—two points, connected by the significant requirement that in both these respects the two sheets be exactly alike. Then follows a more minute specification of two particulars, namely, the number of the loops (the two sheets again corresponding in this, but so obviously that the addition of "likewise" is unnecessary), and their sheet distribution (this latter of course also corresponding with the same item previously stated in another form). To compensate for omitting "likewise" in this verse, the comprehensive remark is subjoined, that when superimposed on each other the two sets absolutely tally. In the case of the more brief but equally accurate account of the roof curtains, on the other hand, we have the corresponding elements of these two propositions relative to each sheet blended, so that there are four facts of resemblance brought out, as before, but not eight, for so many do not here exist. The account, unless *prolix in minutiae* to a degree and in a manner repugnant to this document, must epitomize the account, leaving the reader to make out the meaning by a careful adjustment of all the details and the whole connection.

Accordingly, we have a succinct statement of the number and position of the loops on each sheet, as they appear when the sheets are put together; the color and material—the only different elements—being here taken for granted. Now had the arrangement of the curtains and their loops been so similar as most interpreters make them, the writer would have simply repeated the description of the side curtains (varying, of course, only the circumstances of material, size and number), as he does in other instances of correspondence (for example, in the two altars). Or he would have simply abridged it, as he does in other instances (for example, the several door screens and posts). But he could truthfully do neither, because there were important differences to which he must allude, however briefly; and these are accordingly implied, but not specifically dwelt upon. It is inevitable that these almost-occult distinctions should create ambiguity and puzzle the student. For this very reason we have devoted so much space to their elucidation, as they materially affect the reconstruction; and the conventional modes of disposing of these curtains, especially the colored ones, have led only to hopeless conjectures, false exegesis and impracticable restorations. This part of the structure has truly been the *pons asinorum* of interpreters. We have faithfully tried to guide the unprejudiced reader safely over the quagmire, ourselves thankful to have found so stable footing. We are now prepared, therefore, to present the following as a free version, giving the correct meaning of the two passages in parallel columns.

Side curtains (Exod. 26:4, 5)	*Roof curtains* (Exod. 26:10)
Thou shalt make loops of violet [cord] on the selvedge of the under curtain [-stuff running all along] *past* [each] end [-seam] in the [combined] sheet; and thou shalt do the same on the selvedge of the curtain [-stuff, that runs similarly]	Thou shalt make fifty loops on the selvedge of the under curtain [-stuff, including the corresponding portion of the piece sewed] endwise in the [combined] sheet; and fifty on the selvedge of the curtain [-stuff, which forms] the upper

endwise in the upper [combined] sheet; fifty loops in the under curtain [-stuff], and fifty in the end [-wise] curtain [-stuff] which is in the upper [combined] cloth—the loops to coincide with each other. | [combined] sheet [including in like manner the corresponding portion of the endwise piece].

This completes the system of double house coverings for every closed part of the edifice: a twofold blanket of skins on the outside of the walls, like a weather-boarding; a twofold drapery of linen-and-wool[46] on their inside, like a wainscoting; and a twofold canvas of camlet on the roof and rear gable, like a shingling. All the front coverings were single, as here the structure was strictly a tent. We observe incidentally that both sets of "curtains," although substantially duplicated, as if sufficient for two such structures, are pointedly said (vv. 6, 11) to be so brought together by the knobs as to form "one tent" and one "tabernacle," respectively. This would surely have been an inappropriate remark, if both had been stretched single overhead, as has been done by interpreters from Josephus to our own day. That the dark goat's-hair curtains, and the party colored wool-and-linen ones were not applied to the entire edifice in the same manner is certain from the distinction expressly made everywhere in the sacred text as to their purpose and use. The former constituted the sloping roof and the triangular gables of its "tent" part.[47] No portion of either set was spread horizontally; for the building had no floor but the ground, and no ceiling but the roof. Indeed, as even the English reader will see, a cloth stretched so as to form a horizontal surface is never called a "curtain;" nor in any other position than a vertical one (partly so at least) can it appropriately be said to be "hung." Note, however, that each "covering" of

---

46. Not *linsey-woolsey* (the *shaatnéz* of Lev. 19:19; Deut. 22:11), in which the thread is composed of these two materials carded and spun together.

47. Exod. 26:7, "for a tent [A.V., inexactly "covering"] upon the tabernacle;" v. 11, "couple the tent together;" v. 13, "curtains of the tent;" yet carefully, v. 13, the eave width only of one cubit is to "hang over the sides of the tabernacle;" and v. 12, similarly the rear gable, while the latter adorned the upright walls of the "tabernacle" part (*mishkán*, vv. 1, 6).

skin began at the top, (*millemálah*) on the "tent" part (v. 14), i.e., between the two layers of the roof curtains, although, as it continued downward, of course it was mainly on the upright walls of the tabernacle. The same distinctions are nicely repeated in the subsequent statements (36:8, 13, 14, 18, 19; 40:19).

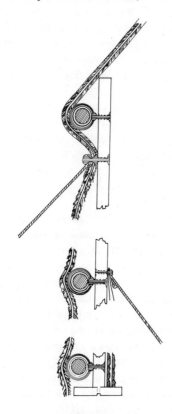

Fig. 15.—Section of wall plank with attachments

A notable dignity, however, is given to these side curtains, beyond the beauty of the doorway curtains so far mentioned, which they otherwise exactly resembled in fabric, by their embroidery of "cherubim of cunning work" (26:1; 36:8), instead of the simple tracery upon the other colored hangings. Leaving the discussion of the form and character of these figures till we meet them as statues over the Ark, we will here consider how the curtains themselves were adapted to so bold a delineation. Imagine the depicting of such awfully mysterious objects in all varieties of incongruous and impossible attitudes—some aslant, some horizontal, some actually upside down, all over the ceiling and walls of a sanctum like this! Yet that would certainly result from the position ordinarily assigned these tapestries, unless the figures were embroidered upon them so displayed as to appear upright. If they had been worked upon the festooned part of the curtains they must have looked as if decapitated. This shows the necessity, when reproducing the Tabernacle in a manner that could be operated, of taking into account a multitude of considerations not usually thought of.

The special emphasis laid upon the injunction, "See that thou make all things according to the pattern shown thee in the Mount," as well as its repetition on several occasions (Exod. 25:9, 40; 26:30; Num. 8:4), shows that many minor details were left out of the oral description to be supplemented by that ocular exhibit. Interpreters are therefore warranted and even required to exercise their ingenuity in discovering the most natural, simple, consistent and effectual mode of supplying these particulars. It is not sufficient for them, any more than it was for the original fabricators, to say that the thing was doubtless done in some suitable way; the precise manner must be pointed out or else conjecturally adopted.

As the curtains were each twice as long as the entire circuit of the three walls, they must in some way have been gathered in (for the straight lines characteristic of the building and especially of all the other hangings, are not in accord with festoons; nor will the thick and firm material admit of these). The heavy and hard ("double-twisted") thread of the linen warp (which, it should be noted, *took all the strain,* and this was very considerable, especially in the door screens; certainly causing them to sag greatly but for this fact) would partly bury itself in the looser texture of the woollen woof (which is not said to be "double-stranded," as it would in that case have been too thick), but would at the same time materially stiffen these threads also. We may, furthermore, observe that the under course of the side curtains would exactly follow the folds of the outer one, and thus aid in maintaining them in a graceful shape. Finally, the embroidered figures would greatly stiffen the panels. We may add that the droop at the bottom of the fulled-in part of the curtains would not be sufficient to account for the difference between their height and that of the Veil, even if the folds included the whole excess of length (i.e., without any flat panels); so that long loops would in any case be necessary.

The problem is how to arrange the folds in such a manner as to exhibit the cherubim perfectly and in a becoming posture. They would naturally be embroidered crosswise of the cloth, like the different-colored bands, and would thus show standing, as the width of the stuff (somewhat over six feet) would conveniently correspond to their height (supposing them to have substantially a human form). Hence it is important that the folds of the curtain should be disposed regularly, so that the "fulling in" would conceal and distort the figures as little as possible. We presume that the cherubim were embroidered only on the outer curtain, as they could not be seen on the inner one. If, however, it be thought necessary to have the two precisely alike, this may be effected by simply reversing the order for the inner set of curtains; the figures then appearing on the face next to the wall, and beginning at the southern front, where they fall exactly in due place under those of the outer curtain as above detailed. (See Fig. 16.)

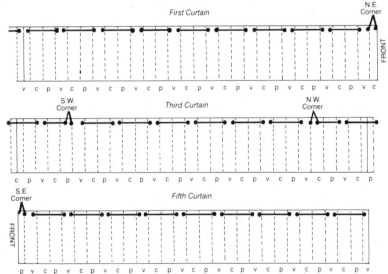

Fig. 16.—Wall curtains extended and furnished with loops

Three of the curtains only, those at the beginning, the middle and the end of the series exposed to view, are here exhibited. The intermediate ones (the second and the fourth) may easily be imagined, as they are of similar character. The letters "v," "p," and "c" designate the *violet,* the *purple,* and the *crimson* stripes respectively, which read after the Hebrew order from right to left.

If the loops be made of pieces of cord each $2\frac{1}{4}$ cubits long (those in the corners proportionately less), with the ends fastened on the selvedge the same distance apart for each cord (so as to open flat with the cloth), and an interval of $\frac{5}{6}$ of a cubit between the ends of adjoining cords, it will be found[48] that fifty loops will exactly take up the entire one hundred forty[49] cubits of each curtain sheet, including four corner loops each occupying $\frac{5}{12}$ of a cubit at the ends and middle; while the folds will (except at the corners) each be $\frac{5}{6}$ of a cubit wide (when hung), with a nearly smooth panel of the same width between them, sufficient for a cherub with folded arms and wings, or for the body of one with the wings extended. It will moreover be perceived that the loops, if so adjusted, will of themselves hold the plaits in good shape, when the curtains are hung on

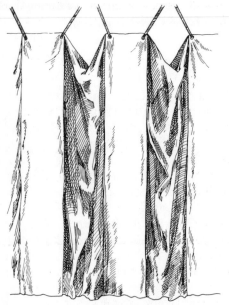

Fig. 17.—Arrangement of side curtain

48. We have proved this estimate by actual experiment, and we will (below) confirm it in a striking manner.

49. This number of itself, being exactly twice the circuit of three sides of the interior of the Sanctuary, suggests that the curtains in question were intended to be so applied. The degree of their fulness, however, remains to be accounted for.

the knobs. They will also show much better with their ends parted into a triangle than if hanging straight down from the knobs. The two folds adjoining each corner will require less cloth for a proportionate degree of fulling, on account of the narrow spaces there afforded, as we shall see presently; but they will project about as much as their neighbors. The careful reader will, furthermore, discover that the reduction of these shorter plaits near the corners, together with the omission of one entire plait (but not one loop) in the very corner, precisely accounts for the fact that the cubits in the length of the curtains are less than three times the number of loops (140 not 150), although each plait (with the alternate panel) requires three cubits of cloth. This is proved by a short calculation. An irregular knob being set in the rear edges of the last side plank (in order to prevent the curtain from passing the corner diagonally, without penetrating to the angle itself), instead of the adjoining side plank (there being none such), there is a loss there (with respect to the space usually covered) of $\frac{1}{6}$ of a cubit (i.e., twice the distance of the knob from the edge, which we put down as $\frac{1}{12}$ of a cubit. In like manner there is a loss of half a cubit in the rear part of the corner plank ($\frac{3}{4} - \frac{3}{12}$), the last item being the half cubit of the rear plank that shows inside, minus the three spaces usually allowed for the knobs from the edge of these three consecutive planks, which here are not saved. Hence we have the formula: $3 \times 2(1 + \frac{1}{3} + \frac{1}{2} = 1\frac{2}{3}) = 10$. We are the first to explain fully and satisfactorily the cause of this exact length of these curtains, which is so singular among the other numbers and dimensions of the edifice, and especially different from that of the roof curtains. In Fig. 19 we submit another mathematical demonstration of its accuracy.

Finally, we may call attention to the fact, under this arrangement, that the edge of the curtains at the entrance will fall back a little farther from the front edge of the first plank than if the loops hung perpendicularly, and this is desirable in order to keep it out of the weather; and this again will allow a closer juxtaposition of the doorpost to the sidewall, as is helpful in order to keep the former from swaying, since they are not fastened together by a hook (as in the case of the Veil). (The following diagrams will illustrate these

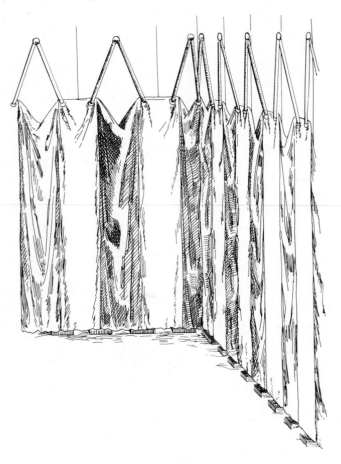

Fig. 18.—Corner folds in wall curtains

measurements, and the method of forming the plaits.) Hence the curtains were not so long as those intended for the roof, which, if attached to each other in the same manner, would each yield ten cubits more than can be thus disposed of.

The curtains were evidently meant to be "fulled in" to exactly half their entire length. The folds on the inside of the planks thus correspond, by their corrugation, to the fleece on the outside; and in both instances, as already pointed out, they are duplicated.

The number of loops was determined by that of the knobs on which they were suspended; namely, fifty of gold (v. 6), and therefore smaller than those of copper for the outside of the planks, and inserted lower down, but in all other respects exactly corresponding

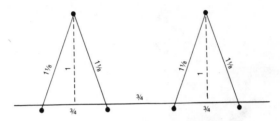

Fig. 19.—Length of side-loops by triangulation
The numbers indicate the proportion of the parts of the triangles

to them. The number of the knobs again was fixed by that of the planks, and is therefore twenty for each side, six for the rear, and two for each corner, requiring the total of fifty, the knobs (except at the corners) being placed as near as convenient to the front edge of each side plank, and in the middle of each rear plank. This calculation serves likewise for the copper knobs on the outside, except that the loops will there be shorter, and both ends of each fastened together, so as to form simple button-holes (so to speak) closely clasping the knobs, and stretching the curtain perfectly smooth. It must be borne in mind that in both sets of knobs, two will be needed in each corner plank, one at the front edge, and another at the angle, in order to keep the curtain uniform. This brings the inside corner knobs nearer their neighbors, as already taken into account. (See Figs. 11, 16.) The height of these knobs from the ground fixes the length of the loops and will be determined when we come to consider that of the inner Veil.

The only other articles mentioned as essential to be placed within the front apartment or Holy Place were three, which we will here consider in detail.

The Table of Shewbread

The first of these on the right or north side (probably about midway) was the Table of Shewbread (Exod. 40:22). It was made of acacia-wood, two cubits long, one wide, and one and one half high,[50] overlaid (doubtless the entire surface when put together)

Fig. 20.—Table of Shewbread on the Arch of Titus

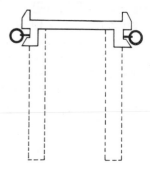

Fig. 21.—Transverse section of the Table of Shewbread

with gold (25:23, 24; 37:10, 11). As a table it consisted, of course, of a top, sides, and four legs; the first of the given length and width, exclusive of an ornament to be considered immediately; and the last of the given dimensions, less the thickness of the top. This last we may estimate at somewhat less than what we have assumed for the boards of the large Altar, let us say $\frac{1}{12}$ of a cubit (about $1\frac{1}{2}$ inch stuff). The top had a "crown"[51] or molding of gold (apparently

---

50. Literally *table of the Face* (i.e., Jehovah's presence), or *table of the arrangement* (of loaves), or *the pure table* (in distinction from a domestic or common one).

This proportion between the length and the height is accurately maintained in the sculptured form on the Arch of Titus. Oriental tables, it should be remembered, are usually quite low, being adapted to persons sitting on the floor, and not upon chairs.

51. Hebrew *zer*, lit. *cincture*, i.e., cornice; used only of this ornament on the Table and the Ark, and the Incense Altar. The great Altar had no occasion for this additional rim, as it had no top or cover. The "cove" (or hollowed bevel) of the molding, of course, was on the upper and outer side, making a neat finish all around the edge.

wood, plated with gold), evidently running all around the edge but outside of the latter, and projecting above the top, to keep articles placed upon the table from slipping off. We may estimate this piece as the same thickness (at the base, narrowing to one half at the top), and $\frac{1}{6}$ of a cubit (or about three inches) broad (i.e., projecting one half its width above the table-top).

The sides are called "a border"[52] or plain panel, being a hand-breadth ($\frac{1}{6}$ of a cubit) wide, and ornamented by another "crown" or molding (this time likewise projecting out like the other, and similarly placed, but narrower, so as to be flush with the bottom of the side, and therefore included in its width), both plated with gold (25:25). The legs or "feet" (which we would make $\frac{1}{6}$ of a cubit square, their whole length), were apparently mortised into the sides. The remaining directions concerning a carrying apparatus (precisely like that of the large Altar, except that gold was to be used instead of copper), the rings, evidently stapled like those of the Tabernacle planks, are spoken of as being fastened into the tops belonging to (A.V. incorrectly "on") the legs, and simply parallel with ("over against," i.e., longitudinally in a line with) the sides (25:26, 27). The whole table, like all the other pieces of furniture, was simple and plain as possible, and strong for service.

The bread placed upon the table is called in the Hebrew *face bread* (shewbread), because it was set as before Jehovah's presence (v. 30). Particulars concerning this are given in Leviticus 24:5-9. It was made of fine wheat flour, doubtless unleavened, but beaten up light, baked in twelve loaves,[53] containing each one fifth of an

---

52. Hebrew *misgéreth*, lit. *enclosure;* used only (as an architectural term) of this thing, and of a similar panel on the pedestals of the Temple lavers (1 Kings 7:28-36; 2 Kings 16:17).

53. A.V. "cakes," Hebrew sing. *challáh*, lit. *perforated* (affording color to the idea that it was punctured, as sacrificial cakes were among some ancient nations. Or more likely, as is often done by modern bakers, who prick biscuits, partly for ornament, and partly because the steam is supposed to escape the more easily in baking), used only of sacrificial cakes (or as in 2 Sam. 6:19, of something resembling them). Therefore, it was not the ordinary thin wafer-like loaf of Oriental bread, yet doubtless round and flat, but much thicker and more daintily put up. The best idea of these cakes is perhaps afforded by similar sacred loaves

ephah of flour (or about four quarts), which, if as spongy as good raised bread, would yield an enormous bulk, but probably, being more compact, was much less in size, say twelve inches in diameter and four inches thick—still a large family loaf.[54] They were arranged "(in) two rows, six (to) the row."[55] which Jewish tradition, as well as the dimensions of the table, indicates to mean in two piles of six each, set, of course, lengthwise of the table; and thus if the piles were in immediate contact with one another (as the necessity of mutual support in so tall a column, and the close association of the twelve tribes thereby symbolized, would indicate), they would leave a free margin of four and one half inches at each side, and nine inches at each end (exactly proportional to the respective dimensions of the table surface, and the whole a shapely mass two feet long, two high, and one foot wide). It is generally conceded that the loaves were placed upon the bare table, without any plate or cloth. They were removed every Sabbath to be eaten by the priests exclusively (and that in the Sanctuary only); and were then replaced by fresh loaves (1 Sam. 21:6), which had been prepared overnight by the Levites (1 Chron. 9:32).

No other substance[56] is mentioned as being set upon the table, except "pure"[57] frankincense, which, as it is said to be placed "upon each [lit. "the"] row,"[58] but only "to [or "for"] the bread" (v. 7, where the A.V. incorrectly renders the latter preposition "on"), appears to

---

represented on the Egyptian monuments (see Wilkinson, *Ancient Egyptians,* i, 266, where nearly all the articles and utensils enumerated in the Scripture list as belonging to the Table of Shewbread are depicted). We must be on our guard, however, against supposing that these are the models of those in the Tabernacle.

54. Five of them were sufficient for hungry David and his companions, perhaps for several meals (1 Sam. 21:1-6).

55. Hebrew *maaréketh,* lit. *arrangement,* used only of this particular thing, and hence (as seen above) taken at last to denote it technically.

56. A dish of *salt* appears to have been added in later times, according to the Septuagint and Philo (comp. Lev. 2:13, which, however, refers to sacrifices on the Altar of Burnt-offering).

57. Hebrew *zak,* unadulterated, like the transparent oil used for the candelabrum (Lev. 24:2).

58. We observe incidentally that this confirms the above arrangement of the loaves in piles.

have been deposited not directly upon the loaves themselves, but in vessels for that purpose, where it could be conveniently renewed as fast as it should be consumed by the daily ministrations at the Altar of Incense (v. 7). These vessels are doubtless the same as the censers[59] (mentioned in the same connection, A.V. "spoons"), i.e., incense-cups, not employed for burning the incense in, which was done in fire-pans, and moreover this was merely frankincense, but smaller than the receptacles of the same name presented by the phylarchs at the dedication (Num. 7:14 and following) for keeping the incense in bulk.

A different set of utensils connected with the Table were jars[60] (A.V. "dishes"), evidently for the oil used to replenish the candelabrum adjacent, similar to the larger silver vessels of the same name (A.V. "chargers") presented by the phylarchs on the above occasion, which also contained oil (Num. 7:13, etc.). They probably were tall vessels with a narrow mouth for emptying. Another kind of utensil were jugs[61] (A.V. "covers"), which, as they were used to make libations with, were doubtless for wine,[62] with a spout for pouring; and closely connected with them were still a different class of vessels, perhaps smaller pitchers[63] (A.V. "bowls"), for the immediate sacrificial act. None of these vessels seems to have had either handle or cover, although most of them might be thought to require closing in order to keep out flies, dust and other impurities; and especially the incense cups, to prevent evaporation of the aromatic powder. It must be borne in mind, however, that a cover would be inconvenient for the priest to remove, and the vessels appear to

59. Hebrew sing. *kaph*, lit. the *palm* of the hand, a saucer.

60. Hebrew sing. *keäráth*, lit. *deep* vessels, spoken only of this article, mentioned above and in the parallel list, Num. 4:7.

61. Hebrew sing. *kasáh*, lit. a *round* vessel, spoken only of this article as mentioned in these passages and in 1 Chron. 28:17 (A.V. "cups").

62. Wine was poured out as a libation (heb. *nések*, a *pouring*, A.V. "drink-offering," as unfortunate a rendering as "meat offering" for an oblation of flour) in connection with many sacrifices on the great Altar. To drink wine within the sacred precincts was a capital crime (Lev. 10:9).

63. Hebrew sing. *menakkíth*, lit. *libation* cups, occurring only of this article in this passage and in Jer. 52:19.

have been intended to hold only a comparatively small quantity at a time.

The saucers for the frankincense would diffuse a pleasant odor during the week, and what was left in them was burned (on the great Altar) every Sabbath (vv. 7-9), together with what was not eaten of the stale loaves. Indeed there was not room for large utensils on the Table, but as there would appear to have been but two (the plural is used of them all) of each kind (that number being stated with regard to the incense cups, which, however, were set on the top of the piles of bread), we may readily accommodate one of each of the three other kinds on either end of the Table. The two bowl-shaped utensils depicted as standing upon the Table of Shewbread on the Arch of Titus at Rome are regarded by Edersheim[64] as the mortars used for compounding the sacred incense. If intended to represent the vessels for oil and wine regularly set on the table, they are of a much later pattern than those of the Tabernacle. All the vessels were of entirely pure gold, as was the overlaying of the Table itself, and indeed all the gold employed in the Sanctuary and its apparatus. Some alloy (to harden the metal) might be necessary in the plates of the Tabernacle walls, which were subject to great wear.

Altar of Incense

The next piece of furniture that we meet in glancing around the Holy Place is the Altar of Incense, that stood in the middle line, immediately in front of the Veil that separated the room from the Most Holy (Exod. 30:6; 40:5; Lev. 16:18), a position which is further proved by the fact that incense was daily offered upon it by an ordinary priest (Exod. 30:7-10), whereas the Holy of Holies was entered but once a year by the high priest alone. Yet it was popularly reckoned as belonging to the Most Holy Place (1 Kings 6:22; Heb. 9:4), apparently on account of its great sanctity.

In construction (Exod. 30:1-5; 37:25-28) it was very similar to the Table of Shewbread, being a simple box (probably of boards of the same thickness), two cubits high, with a top (destitute of a grate, because no fire came directly in contact with it), one cubit square,

---

64. Edersheim, Alfred, *The Temple and its Services,* p. 134.

and horns (precisely like the large Altar); and was entirely overlaid with gold (doubtless inside and out). It had a molding around the edge (but none below this), and rings with staves to carry it, exactly like the Table of Shewbread. From the fact that the rings in this case are stated to have been set "beneath the molding corners," which is not said of the other pieces of furniture so equipped, we conclude that there was a slight space between them in those cases, but none in this. The reason for this difference was not simply because the Altar of Incense was the smallest, but because the Table of Shewbread had *two* such moldings, and the bar would be symmetrically placed halfway between them; while the great Altar had no molding at all. In the case of the Ark, although it had but one molding, and that in the same place as the others, yet the staples for the rings would have come so near the upper edge of the side (not there strengthened by a top fastened to them), as to be in danger of tearing away the wood, especially since the heavy stone tables of the Law were to be carried inside. There were no utensils specially belonging to the Altar of Incense. The only use made of it was to burn incense upon it every morning and evening.

Candelabrum

On the left or south side of the Holy Place, directly opposite the Table of Shewbread (Exod. 40:24),[65] stood the third piece of furniture; namely, the Candelabrum (A.V. "candlestick"), the construction of which is minutely described (25:31-40; 37:17-24). It was hammered round,[66] out of sheets[67] of pure gold, and weighed (inclusive of its utensils) one talent (i.e., 136.4 pounds avoirdupois).

65. From this language, in the absence of any explicit statement, as well as from the congruity with the dimensions of the room, and with convenience in serving, we conclude that the position of both these pieces of furniture was with their length running east and west.

66. Hebrew *mikshâh* (A.V., "beaten work"), which seems lit. to mean *rounded,* like a pillar (Jer. 10:5, A.V. "upright"); applied also to the silver trumpets (A.V. "of one" or a "whole piece") and to the cherubim on the Mercy Seat.

67. The parts might perhaps have been cast as plain tubes, but they could then not have been wrought into shape, for no anvil could have been introduced into their sinuosities.

The mode of its manufacture indicates that it was hollow, and Josephus affirms that this was the case.[68] Its size is not given, but Jewish tradition assigns it a height of about five feet, and a width of about $3\frac{1}{2}$. On the Arch of Titus it measures two feet and nine inches high by two feet wide. The figures there delineated, however, are not life size, and the proportion with the Table of Shewbread on the same sculpture, as well as with the men there exhibited, yields a size about the same as the above tradition. We may, therefore, fix the entire height (including the base) at about three cubits, and the entire breadth (spread of arms) at about two cubits. This would be suitable to its location and use. As to its general form, the principal question is, whether the arms were in the same plane and of equal height. This may be regarded as settled in the affirmative by the

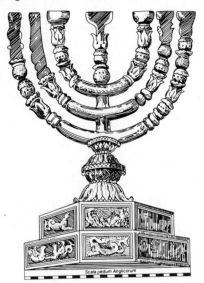

Fig. 22.—Candelabrum on the Arch of Titus

Fig. 23.—Concentric arrangement of the enlargements of the Candelabrum[69]

---

68. This view is corroborated by the term (Heb. *kanéh*, lit. a *reed*) used for the "branches." (See Josephus, *Antiquities of the Jews,* III, vi, 7.)

69. It will be perceived that each section of the semicircles of which these lines

representation on the Arch of Titus, which, although copied from that of the Herodian Temple,[70] is doubtless a correct transcript of the Sinaitic one, except in its ornamental features (especially the octagonal base, with figured panels).

In detail the candelabrum consisted of three parts, each of which was made of a single piece of metal; namely, a straight central stem, three pairs of semicircular branches on either side, and seven burners. Each of the first seven components were a round pipe with

---

are the radii is composed of two members: the shank (a plain tube) and the bulb (or swell), and that each has a third part or base (a circular double flange, as a means of connection, hence an actual joint) only where it is united to a different kind of piece; i.e., at the bottom and top of the central shaft and of the six arms, including the intersections of the shaft with the arms. There were, therefore, exactly ten screwed joints covered by as many caps in the entire piece (exclusive of the seven movable insertions of the lamps in their sockets), namely, the triple one at each of the three intersections (where the ends of the arms passed through the shaft on either side [as the flange or "knop" permitted by widening the neck of the shaft just at that point; at the same time bracing the end of the arm], and were screwed into each other), and the four junctions of the almond-shaped "bowls" with the terminal "flowers." The "knops" or joint-covers are accordingly an integral part of the compound "bowls" or whole pieces, that support the entire segment. If, as we have supposed, the pieces were made of sheets, there would be a seam the whole length of each, which would, of course, be on the back side of the shaft, and on the inner curve of the arms. These might be soldered together (and the screws at the joints likewise be thus dispensed with), if the art of soldering gold were then known.

70. Tradition asserts that this candelabrum, after undergoing various migrations from Rome to foreign lands and back again, was finally lost in the Tiber during an invasion of the Gauls. At all events it is certain that the sculptor must have had the original or a careful drawing of it before him. If it be thought that Titus would scarcely have had time to remove the candelabrum from the Holy Place (although he seems to have done so with the Table of Shewbread) during his hasty survey of the sacred apartments, while the rapid conflagration was in progress (Josephus, *Wars of the Jews,* VI, iv, 7), the one actually rescued and represented on his arch may possibly be one of those which tradition reports as the present of the convert to Judaism, Helena, queen of Adiabene, which were kept in an anteroom of the Temple porch. This may perhaps account for its difference from the Mosaic type. But in any case it must be borne in mind that the postexilian candelabrum was but a reproduction from memory of that in the Tabernacle.

three kinds of ornamental enlargements at certain points, corresponding to each other in a radiate manner. All these elements were substantially represented, in a more ornate style, on the Arch of Titus. Josephus[71] explicitly states that the candelabrum displayed by Titus at his triumph differed considerably in some particulars, but, nevertheless, it must have been substantially of the normal type. The main axis was, no doubt, spread out like a trumpet at the base, in order to give a firm support. It had four bowls (Heb. sing. *gebía,* lit. *curvature*), which were almond-shaped (i.e., the nut [not the blossom, for which this term is never used], or *ovate,* or tapering from a head, like a goblet or wine cup, for which the former word is elsewhere used, Gen. 44:2-17; Jer. 35:5). They are named first as rising immediately from the base and from the three intersections of the branches, and therefore are found (but only three of them) on each branch, also as springing from the intersection like a new base. This appears to be the meaning in Exodus 25:35; 37:21; for if the end of the branch were inserted simply into the stem, it would have cut it entirely in two, both being doubtless of the same diameter. We have therefore inserted the arms into the "flower" (of which, as well as the "knop," there are said to be four [i.e., one at each intersection, and one at the top] in the shaft, but only one in each arm [i.e., at the top]), which affords a sufficient enlargement at the intersection (i.e., not above it [for then there would have been at least two on each arm], nor yet [like the "knops"] below it). (See Fig. 24.)

Next in order on the main shaft at these intersections respectively are the same number of coronets (Heb. sing. *kaphtór,* lit. *chaplet,* A.V. "knop"), i.e., doubly-flaring circlets, like the capital of a column (Amos 9:1; Zeph. 2:14), evidently below the intersection of the branches. They do not appear on the branches themselves (except one at the summit, as a fresh departure), but correspond to the expanded base (a single flange as terminal in this direction).[72] Once more there was a like number of finials (Heb. sing. *pérach,* lit. *blossom,* A.V. "flower"), like a bud just ready to burst into bloom

---

71. Josephus, *Wars of the Jews,* VII, v, 5.

72. The same meaning attaches to the proper name *Caphtor,* from the chaplet-like form of the island Crete or (still better) Cyprus.

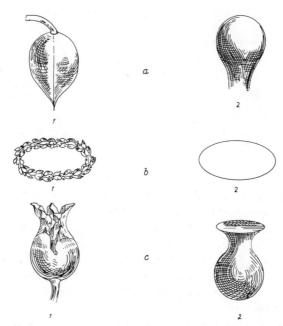

Fig. 24.—Comparison of each of the enlargements on the Candelabrum with its natural type
a. Almond (1) and "bowl" (2)   *b.* Chaplet (1) and "knop" (2)   *c.* "Flower" (1) and bud (2)

(Isa. 5:24; 18:5; Nah. 1:4). Next to them there was an architectural ornament of a like form in the Temple (1 Kings 7:20; 2 Chron. 4:5), i.e., globes or receptacles for the arms and burners. These, which, of course, belong to the branches likewise, we have drawn in a bulb-like form with a corolla, aided by the spherical remains on the Arch of Titus.

Finally come the lamps themselves (Heb. sing. *ner,* lit. a *light,* often used of a "lamp"), which, of course, were of the type universally prevalent in the East: a flat, round or oval dish (usually of terra-cotta, but here of gold), with a handle, like that of a cup, at the blunt end. There was a hole for the wick at the pointed end, while in a depression between is a larger central hole for pouring in the oil. In the present case we presume they were deepened into a cylindrical form at the base in order to fit in the lamp holders at the tops of

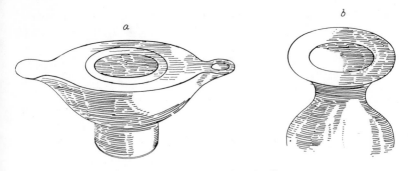

Fig. 25.—Lamp (*a*) and its socket (*b*)

the Candelabrum, and not easily fall off.[73] The wick was made of threads of linen from the cast-off pontifical garments, it is traditionally said, and the oil was from hand crushed and cold strained olives (Exod. 27:20). The lamps were lighted at the time of the evening sacrifice (Exod. 30:8) and extinguished, filled and trimmed at the time of the morning sacrifice (Exod. 30:7; 1 Sam. 3:3). Traditionally, it is believed that each held half a "log," i.e., a little more than half a pint. (See Fig. 25.)

The utensils mentioned for this last-named service, being those already referred to as made out of the same gold as the candlestick itself, were shovels (Heb. sing. *machtáh*, lit. *coal-pan*, A.V. "snuff-dish," being the same word used for the [copper] fire pans of the great Altar, Exod. 27:3, etc.; the [gold] one of the yearly atonement, Lev. 16:12; and "censers" generally), i.e., vessels used to bring live coals from the great Altar; and tongs (Heb. always dual, *malkachá-yim*, lit. *double takers*), i.e., tweezers for pulling up the wick, and holding the coal while blowing it to light the lamp. These utensils were carried by the officiating priest to the Court, where the tongs would be cleansed, and the coal-pan refilled for further use.

The Silver Trumpets

The only remaining articles belonging to the Holy Place are the

---

73. Such seem to be represented on the monuments of Egypt (Wilkinson, *Ancient Egyptians,* ii, 376).

two Silver Trumpets[74] used to announce a removal of the camp, special festivals, the Year of Jubilee, war, or any other other notable event (Num. 10:2-10, etc.), which were to be of a single piece (probably manufactured like the pipes of the Candelabrum). They were straight,[75] as represented on the Arch of Titus, where they are exhibited as about equal to each other in average diameter, but unequal in length, (compared with the dimensions of the Table of Shewbread, on which they are represented as leaning diagonally, supported by a sort of bracket attached for that purpose to the middle of the opposite legs on one side),[76] one was about three cubits long, and the other only $\frac{3}{4}$ as long or about two cubits. The minimum diameter of both is about $\frac{1}{12}$ of a cubit (or $1\frac{1}{2}$ inches, and the maximum $\frac{1}{16}$ of a cubit (or $7\frac{1}{2}$ inches. The longer one tapers almost gradually to about the middle and then slightly enlarges towards the mouth-end, while the shorter one contracts at first rapidly, and after the middle enlarges considerably. This difference in the size of the trumpets is so unexpected, as there is no allusion to it in any record, and it would have occasioned a difference in sound, that we must attribute it to foreshortening in the perspective, which the sculptor introduced, and the camera has enhanced. We, therefore, strike an average of $2\frac{1}{2}$ cubits (about four feet) for the length of each. They would give a clear shrill note loud enough to be heard throughout the camp.

Other Details

We now want to consider here some additional matters connected with all this sacred apparatus.

The metallic sheets, whether of copper or gold, could most conveniently be laid on after the wooden work was put together, and would serve to hold the angles firm. These laminae must have been beaten out with a hammer (in the absence of rolling mills), and

---

74. Hebrew sing. *chatsotseráh,* lit. a quivering *reverberation,* used only for an alarm, or public signal, sometimes of joy.

75. Josephus, *Antiquities of the Jews,* III, xi, 6.

76. Evidently meant for the *front;* an additional confirmation of the position of the Table longitudinally in the Sanctuary.

therefore, have been comparatively small, as well as somewhat uneven in surface. Hence they were probably fastened on with nails of the same material as soldering would have been inconvenient, and was perhaps unknown with such metals. If these were made with countersunk heads, like modern screws, they might be driven home flush with the surface. The numerous joints or seams thus formed would greatly strengthen the fabric. As the boards themselves, especially the planks of the Tabernacle walls which were similarly "overlaid," were so wide that it was necessary that they be made of several pieces of wood, no doubt dowelled together, their joints would thus be effectively covered and held together. The thickness of these metallic plates is likewise left to the feasibility of the case. Fortunately, both copper and gold are the most malleable of the metals then known.

Another inference from the foregoing premises is that the staples for the rings, which received the cross bars of the Tabernacle walls, and the bearing poles of three of the pieces of furniture as well as the "taches" or knobs (in the former), were bolted in and riveted before the "overlaying" sheets were applied. Otherwise, they would likely come in the way of nails, and moreover would be unsightly protuberances on the surface, especially the copper ends of the "taches," showing inside the Sanctuary on the face of the gold. Paine infers, from the special mention of these knobs among the various articles *as completed* (Exod. 39:33), that they were separable, i.e., keyed on the back side, and not riveted fast. This, however, would be an inconvenient circumstance, exposing them to be lost in transportation, and requiring unnecessary waste of time in taking them out and replacing them at each journey. His conclusion that they permanently belonged to the planks, from their constant and close mention together, is forcible. In the personal inventory ("by name," Num. 4:32) of the articles packed and consigned for transportation (3:36), they are not separately enumerated, as are the sockets, the bars, the tent pins and the cords.

TRANSPORTATION

As to convenience in packing for transportation, these rings and knobs would not need to be removed, as the Tabernacle planks would be smooth on the inner side, and thus could lie flat on the bottom of the vehicle. Better still, if the wagon were without a bottom, the planks might be laid face downward on the axle or bolster; and a second tier, face upward, over these. Strips of wood, perhaps covered with cloths or skins, were probably placed between the planks in order to prevent chafing. The tablets and other articles within the Ark were no doubt kept wrapped in linen cloths, which would ease the jolt in moving. The vehicles of the ancients, and especially of the Egyptians, were *carts* with two wheels only, and even these must have had rough travelling in the trackless and often steep as well as tortuous defiles of the desert. A *wagon*,[77] however, with four wheels and two axles, would have been much more suitable for the present purpose, as affording a stable support, and being less liable to jostle and overturn, especially for the long planks and poles. In either case the load would have to be bound together by cordage, and for this the stay ropes would be at hand.

Since the silver sockets alone (to say nothing of the copper ones) weighed six gross tons (100×136.4 pounds), some special mode of conveyance must have been provided for them, beyond the six vehicles appropriated to the wooden and the fibrous parts of the edifice and its court. Perhaps the Kohathites (who were the most numerous of the Levites, and had only the light burden of the sacred vessels) aided their brethren the Merarites (who were the smallest branch of the Levitical tribe, and yet had the heaviest charge) in transporting these weighty but not bulky articles, or possibly ordinary Israelites were subsidized for that purpose. A socket might conveniently be carried by two men with a tent pin thrust through its mortice. The roof posts and the wall bars also, which were too long to be placed upon the wagons, were probably carried by men upon their shoulders. There is no trace of the possession or employment of camels by the Hebrews in this journey, although at present they are the only "ships of the desert" possible by reason of the

---

77. Hebrew *agaláh,* lit. "a *rolling* thing" (Num. 7:3-8), an Egyptian curricle (Gen. 45:19-27), elsewhere rendered "cart," as in fact it generally was.

scarcity of water and the absence of roads. In fact the four wagons assigned for the transportation of the wooden portions of the structure must have been supplemented by extra vehicles, or else have made several trips for the purpose, as a little computation will show. A section of an acacia branch in our possession, $4\frac{1}{2}$ inches in diameter and scarcely one inch in thickness, weighs half a pound, although thoroughly seasoned and free from knots.

Each of the fence posts of the Tabernacle court, therefore, weighed at least fifty pounds ($\frac{5\times20}{2}$), to say nothing of their silver caps and copper tenons; and the sixty posts alone would weigh 3,000 pounds, or about a ton and one half. By a similar calculation each of the wall planks would weigh at least 600 pounds, to say nothing of the gold plating, silver tenons or other metallic attachments; and the whole forty-eight would weigh 28,800 pounds, or about fourteen tons. In order to accommodate the number of wagons, the posts might safely be reduced to one-half the diameter that we have supposed for them, which would make their weight comparatively inconsiderable. In like manner perhaps the planks, so that they would weigh collectively (if only about an inch thick, greatly stiffened by the metal plates) about four tons. The difficulty, however, of providing carriage, where resources (and especially human and animal force) seem to have been so abundant, is too slight to require a disturbance of our estimates or a stinting of the materials. Where six wagons were volunteered, twenty or more, if necessary, could easily be procured.

We may remark that the desert itself supplied this wood in abundance, and the copious store of metals, gems and weaving materials were provided in advance by the divine direction (Exod. 3:22; 11:2) to *ask* these things of the Egyptians (a just demand for their long and severe and unrequited labor), and the latter were only glad to bestow in hopes of hastening the departure of their late serfs (Exod. 12:33-36). These valuables they afterwards freely contributed, as they were of little use for commercial purposes in the desert. The furniture was equipped for carrying by hand, two men for the smaller pieces, four for the larger, and eight for the Altar of Burnt Offering. The utensils might also be carried by hand, for there was no lack of people to serve who, however, had their own tents and baggage to carry. It was also possible that they were reverently packed in some of the curtains and hangings of the Tabernacle or its court, when loaded for the march.

POSITION OF THE TRIBES

In the *camp* the position of the several tribes was as shown on the following diagram (Num 2, 4, 7):

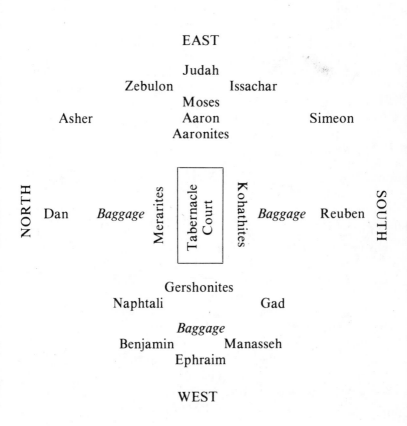

The route pursued was substantially the same as the one usually followed by modern tourists, and presents no insurmountable obstacles, but has several difficult passes. It must be remembered that Moses himself was familiar with the region, and that he had in addition the guidance of his wife's relatives, and especially the everpresent pillar of cloud and fire. A special Providence is intimated at every step and juncture.

On preparing for the *march,* the priests (Aaronites, i.e., sons of Aaron) first took down the Veil and folded it over the Mercy Seat, then wrapped the whole Ark in a blanket of fur kept for this purpose. They covered this again with a sheet of all-wool violet, drawing the side bars into a proper position. Next they covered the Table of Shewbread with a similar woolen cloth, placed all the dishes close around the piles of bread, wrapped the whole in a sheet of all-wool crimson, and covered this again with a fur blanket, putting in the side bars for transportation. Thirdly, they wrapped up the candelabrum and all its apparatus in a sheet of all-wool violet, put the whole in a sack of fur, and hung it on a pole, to be carried in like manner. Fourthly, they wrapped the Altar of Incense in a similar violet sheet, and covered it with a blanket of fur, putting in the bars for carrying it. Fifthly, they wrapped up all the other vessels of the Sanctuary, including the silver trumpets and the golden censers, in a similar violet sheet, and put them in another fur bag for carrying upon a pole. The Laver was doubtless prepared for transportation in like manner. Lastly, they cleared out all the coals and ashes from the Altar of Burnt Offering, spread a purple all-wool cloth over it, set all its copper utensils upon the grate, and then threw a blanket of fur over the whole, putting in the bars for carrying. Not until all this was done did the Levites (of the family of Kohath) approach to take up the pieces of furniture, place the bearing poles on their shoulders, and march away with them. The other Levites then came, took down the court, tent and walls, and packed them on the wagons. The order in the line of march was according to the following diagram, all parties retaining as nearly as possible the relative position of the encampment.

Judah
Issachar
Zebulon

Moses
Aaron
Priests

Dan   Kohathites   Reuben
(*with the furniture on their shoulders*)

Asher   Gershonites   Simeon
(*with the tent-stuff and cordage on two wagons*)

Naphtali   Merarites   Gad
(*with the wooden-work and fixtures on four wagons*)

Ephraim
Manasseh
Benjamin

It may be presumed that the stations enumerated in Exodus 12—19 and Numbers 33 represent only the principal encampments, where the Israelites stopped for a considerable period. The route indicated was that of the *headquarters* only, consisting of the leaders, the families and the ecclesiastical establishment, while the younger men were scattered extensively over the peninsula in charge of the flocks and herds. The pasture appears to have been much more abundant then than now, owing to the stripping of the region of its trees and shrubs (for fuel, especially in the manufacture of charcoal for sale in Egypt), and the consequent drying up of the streams.

THE HOLY OF HOLIES

The inner room, called the Most Holy Place ("holy of holies," a Hebraism), which we may compare to a shrine, was but a continuation of the front room, the walls, roof canvas and side curtains being the same. There are, therefore, but two objects of special consideration here.

The only division between the rooms was another screen, entirely similar to that of the outer doorway, except in one particular, and therefore requiring discussion only as to two points, in which it will be found highly determinative, as its name in the original implies (Heb. *paróketh,* lit. a *separation,* i.e., partition; applied only to this one piece of drapery). It is particularly described in Exodus 26:31-33 and 36:35, 36).

This differed from that of the doorway of the Holy Place in one respect only. It was an embroidery of cherubim instead of plain figures, resembling in this feature the side curtains, except that these were doubtless depicted with extended wings touching each other requiring but two figures to fill the space,[78] for the cloth was, like the other screens, stretched tight and therefore its length needed not to be mentioned, as the space was the entire width of the room.

It was suspended, like the other doorway screens, upon pillars. They were made and furnished exactly like those of the front room, except that their sockets (and of course their tenons also) were of silver instead of copper. They do not appear to have had any connecting rods. The reason for this last difference is that the curtain was fastened, not only by gold hooks in the pillars, but also, *to the side planks.* Thus the whole line was kept from swaying transversely to the building. The pillars, moreover, were four instead of five, as in the case of the front door, because no central one was required to sustain the peak here, and the end ones did not need to touch the wall for their support. We, therefore, presume that they were placed with equal distances between them and also between them and the walls; thus making five spaces of two cubits each from center to center, less $\frac{1}{8}$ cubit for the spaces adjoining the walls. We prefer this method of distribution to that which places them in contact with the walls, leaving three spaces only; because in that

---

78. From 1 Kings 6:23, 24, it appears that the spread of a cherub's wings was reckoned as equal to the whole height of the figure. Hence these two cherubs touching each other with outstretched wings would leave an exactly equal margin on the Veil at the bottom and sides, supposing them to be placed just as far from the top as on the side curtains, where they would seem to have been set in the middle of the widths.

plan the passageways to the Holy of Holies, where a single man passed but once a year, are made wider than those of the front doorway through which many persons must have passed together often every day. The passageways are thus found to contract at every successive enclosure from without inward, as propriety demands. We will find another and more conclusive reason for this arrangement, when we come to consider the succession of colors on the wall drapery.

The position of this inner Veil becomes important, in the first place, for the obvious reason that the dimensions of the two rooms as to length are indicated only by this dividing line, and yet its location in this respect is not expressly stated at all. We are left to the presumption that the inner room was a square, and the outer one twice as long as broad. These conclusions are certified by the proportions of the corresponding apartments in the Temple, as all agree. This will make the dividing line fall at two-thirds of the width of the seventh plank from the rear, and a hook must therefore be inserted at that point in the side walls for that purpose. The presumption is that the posts on which the Veil hung were wholly within the Most Holy Place (i.e., the screen on their outer face, as in both the other cases).

There is but one other suggestion in the text concerning the position of the Veil, and the value or necessity of giving it (which is done in the most explicit terms, as if something important) does not appear until after close study. It is this: "And thou shalt hang up [lit. "give," i.e., *place*] the Veil under the taches [i.e., knobs of the side curtains]" (Exod. 26:33). Since it is not said how much below the knobs the Veil is to be set, the legitimate inference is that it is to be put *immediately* beneath them as in other instances (Exod. 25:35; 26:19; 30:4), whereas an interval, if any, is always indicated by a different expression (Exod. 26:12, 25; 27:5). Observe also that the language is, "under the knobs," i.e., their line in general, not under any particular knob. It should further be noted that this special command concerning the Veil could not have been given for the purpose of fixing its location or dimensions, since it really does not accomplish this in any direction; nor for the main purpose of indicating the height of the knobs from the ground. It was intended rather to point out some peculiarity in the *mode of suspending* the Veil, different from that of the other screens, at the two ends at least, namely, by a hook in the planks themselves, and not in the posts as elsewhere.

We have assumed that the hangings of the interior doorways, namely, of the Holy and the Most Holy places, were uniform in height with those of the outer court, i.e., five cubits (Exod. 38:18), inasmuch as they were all for a like purpose of screening from ordinary view. In the case of the Veil, this is specially confirmed by the parallel height of the golden knobs, which could not well have been lower, if they were to furnish an adequate point of attachment for the interior stay ropes, nor higher, if these last were not to encroach inconveniently upon the margin required about the furniture. The triangulation of the colored loops (Fig. 19) also corroborates the same conclusion.

It must be borne in mind that the side curtains are only four cubits wide (i.e., high, when hung), while the Veil is five cubits. The knobs, therefore, must have been set in the planks one cubit above the upper edge of the curtains. The direction in question reveals to us two interesting facts. First, the Veil was directly attached to the walls, but not to the knobs for, as we have seen, a knob does not fall at the right spot; nor could the Veil be buttoned conveniently or securely upon one, had it been at the place, for it would not project in the proper direction. Secondly, the loops were of such a length that the top of the curtains came one cubit lower than the knobs. The diagram (Fig. 19) shows how mathematically true this would be in the manner of hanging the curtains which we have noted.

There yet remains a still more crucial test of the accuracy and consistency of our method of disposing of these colored curtains. As the full planks are each one and one-half cubits wide, with a knob and a loop to each, and as the joined sheets are each twice as long as the entire circuit of the planks, it follows that every looped portion assigned to a plank must be three cubits long, which allows exactly one cubit for each of the component stripes of color. Now since the flat panels of violet, containing the figure of the cherubim, are each to be five-sixths of a cubit wide between the ends of the loops that stretch them out, or a full cubit including the loops and their eyelets, there are left two cubits for the other two colors, one on each slope of the intervening fold of cloth.

Again, as the entire length of each of the combined sheets is 140 cubits, a number not divisible by three without a remainder, it follows that, if the stripes were woven uniformly in each separate (or uncombined) curtain width (as we cannot doubt they were), at least one of the colors must have fallen short or been redundant at one end or the other. The same conclusion results from the fact that each of these original or separate curtain pieces of stuff was twenty-eight cubits long, giving nine full series of colors (9×3=27), and a surplus cubit for an entire stripe. Let us now suppose that the stripes begin at the front edge of the north planks, and proceed regularly along the walls (after the Hebrew order of reading, as elsewhere observed), in the invariable succession of colors as enunciated in the sacred text, until they terminate at the front edge of the south wall. In order to bring the violet about the middle of the first plank (a position required as that of the embroidered panel, with its connected violet loops), let us commence with the color immediately preceding, i.e., the crimson. We do this with a *half stripe,* instead of a whole one, in accordance with our uniform custom in the case of the door screens. (This half-stripe of crimson, be it noted, is hidden by the door pillar at that point, so that the series will appear to begin in fact with the violet stripe, the one always mentioned first in the textual order of enumeration.) The succeeding purple stripe, together with half the following crimson one, completes the drapery for the first plank, the whole being in entire symmetry, panel and loops properly adjusted to the knob, and commencing as well as ending with a half stripe of the same color.

The series goes on regularly, until we reach the end of the first piece of cloth, which terminates with a half stripe of violet at the middle of the tenth plank. The second piece of stuff, resuming the same series with another half stripe of violet, carries on the order regularly again to the end of this piece, terminating with a half stripe of purple at the last third of the nineteenth plank. The third piece of cloth takes up the same order with another half stripe of purple, which, together with half the adjoining stripe of crimson completes that plank, and the corner reaches in like manner by the first half of the next crimson stripe, the middle of each plank thus far being in every instance covered by the violet panel. Here the half cubit of the rear corner plank changes the adjustment, the remaining half stripe of crimson making the short fold at the corner (without any intervening flat panel). The succeeding violet stripe carries on the series across the joint of the planks to the next fold, which consists of the purple and the crimson stripes falling under the knob in the middle of the first full rear plank, as it should. This last arrangement will continue regularly till the other corner plank is reached in like manner by the last half of the eighth violet stripe of the third curtain piece. Half the adjoining purple one makes the short fold for that plank, precisely as has been done in the opposite corner. The remainder of the purple stripe, together with the whole of the succeeding crimson makes up the (somewhat short) fold on the first (i.e., rear) third of the twentieth south plank (reckoned from the front of the building). Here the next violet stripe once more falls in the middle of a side plank, exactly corresponding to its fellow on the opposite side of the room, and the same arrangement regularly continues for every other side plank to the front corner. The third curtain piece terminates with a crimson half-stripe at the rear third of the nineteenth plank, the fourth piece with a violet half-stripe at the front third of the tenth plank, and the fifth piece with a purple half-stripe at the extremity of the line (hidden by the other door pillar). Thus, the reversal of the order of the stripes on the opposite sides of the rooms is so compensated by the change in the panels at the corners that strict regularity is maintained throughout the entire series, and yet complete correspondence in the position of the twenty violet cherubim-panels on each side, and the seven at the end.

Once more, the Veil, being twenty cubits from the front, and ten cubits from the rear of the interior, falls at the end of the first third of the fourteenth plank from the entrance ($13\frac{1}{2} \times 1\frac{1}{2} = 20$), or, what is the same thing, at the end of the second third of the seventh plank from the end ($6\frac{1}{2} \times 1\frac{1}{2} = 10$). This point will be at the junction of a crimson with a violet stripe on the north side, and of a purple with a violet one on the south side. In both cases, it is immediately in front of the fourteenth violet or cherub panel from the entrance where, be it noted, we have placed no pillar to hide it. This will give exactly seven cherubim to each side, and the same number to the rear of the Most Holy Place, and fourteen to each side and adjoining half of the Veil in the Holy Place, while the two on the Mercy Seat correspond to the two on the Veil; in no instance a cherub on two colors at once. Moreover, if the Veil itself be made to consist of two broad stripes (purple and crimson) for its two cherubim, respectively, with a half stripe of violet on either edge like all the other door screens, this will complete the circuit of the colors continuously in their uniform order around the three sides of the Holy Place, as well as those of the Most Holy.

We are entitled to regard this marvellous series of perfect coincidences in the symmetry and congruity of the scheme which we have propounded for the adjustment of this set of variegated wall curtains, no less than that of the plain roof curtains, as a demonstration of its truth. Novel as it really is, and complicated as it may at first sight appear, it must in the end carry conviction with all who will take the pains to trace it out. When the great Kepler published the volume in which he promulgated his famous "laws" of the mathematical proportions existing between the motions and distances of the planetary bodies, that have since become the basis of all exact calculations in astronomy, he is said to have uttered the memorable words, "I can well afford to wait even centuries, if need be, for an appreciative reader of my theories, since God has waited 6,000 years for an intelligent observer of his universe." In the same spirit of reverent confidence, albeit on a much humbler scale, we may be allowed to claim for our discoveries in regard to this piece of the divine handicraft, that we can equally well afford to wait for a few years, if we must, for an adoptive student of our theory, since Moses has waited more than three millennia for a consistent expositor of his inspired account of the sacred Tabernacle.

At length we have reached the most sacred of all the *penetralia* of the Tabernacle, which doubtless occupied the exact center of the Holy of Holies but a different spot in the Temple (1 Kings 8:8). This sole piece of furniture was the Ark, probably standing transversely in the area so as to exhibit to the best advantage its several parts, which are described in Exodus 25:10-22 and 37:1-9.

The Mercy Seat

In construction the Ark was altogether similar to the other acacia wood boxes which we have already considered, being two and one half cubits long, one and one half wide, and one and one half high (external dimensions), plated with gold inside and out, including the bottom and the top. This last, called the "Mercy Seat" (Heb. *kappóreth,* lit. a *covering,* but not in the figurative sense of *expiation;* hence used only of this article), was in fact a movable *lid,* of the same size as the Ark itself, and thus proved to have shut inside of the molding-cornice ("crown"), which it had, like the other boxes, and of course flush with it, on the upper surface. It was likewise furnished with the usual apparatus for transportation, in the form of gold rings and gold-cased bars. In this case they fitted together tightly, so as never to be removed, which convenience for daily use was required in the other cases. The bars were not to be removed from the rings of the Ark because of its superior sanctity, which forbade all unnecessary handling (see 2 Sam. 6:6, 7). There was not the same occasion for ready passage about it when at rest, as in the case of the other pieces of furniture similarly equipped. The golden censer, with which the high priest once a year only entered the Most Holy Place, was doubtless set upon this lid.

The Cherubim

Upon this lid also, near either end, were placed those most remarkable objects, the Cherubim, which are occasionally referred to in the Scriptures. They are first mentioned in the account of the expulsion from Eden (Gen. 3:24), where they have the emphatic prefix of the article (*the* cherubs, unfortunately neglected in the

A.V.), as if already well known. In fact they must have been, especially to the Israelites, who were familiar with the representation of such figures on the Egyptian monuments. The winged animals of the Assyrian sculptures are also imaginary creatures of a like symbolical character, no doubt, but more gross in their conception. Our chief information concerning scriptural cherubim, besides the passages here discussed, is drawn from the visions of Ezekiel 10 and 40, in which they figure conspicuously, and with a few hints in Isaiah 6. The forms in the account of Solomon's Temple (1 Kings 6:23-29; 2 Chron. 3:10-13) and Ezekiel's (41:18-20), although of colossal size, are doubtless consistent with those in Exodus. The living creatures of the Apocalypse (Rev. 4:6-9) are but reproductions of them. It is noteworthy that the large cherubim of the Temple, mentioned above, are two in number, apparently corresponding to those on the Veil, and not to those on the Ark, which were there also. Those on the Temple walls were in like manner the representatives of the former embroideries on the side curtains.

It is a curious corroboration of our disposal of them in panels with a fold between, that the Temple wainscoat was carved with alternate cherubim and palm trees (Ezek. 41:18), the palm trees taking the place of the fold, which could not well be imitated in wood carving. For artistic effect, the head is there somewhat turned, so as to fairly show two adjoining faces only; and, of course, the nobler ones are selected. The identity of the "living creatures" of Ezekiel with the cherubim is evinced by the fact that under both names they are represented as supporting the triumphal cart of the Almighty (2 Sam. 22:11; Ezek. 1:26; 9:3; 10:1, 4). They both had wheels connected with them (Ezek. 1:15; 10:9); were entirely similar in form (Ezek. 1:10; 10:14, where the ox face is called a cherub face, because the figure had a bovine leg and foot); and in Ezekiel 10:20, they are expressly identified. We have, in this part of our work, to consider only their material form and their posture, leaving their symbolical significance to a later chapter.

The statues, for they were such in the present case, were hammered out (the same word is used as in prescribing the Candelabrum) of sheets of pure gold. Therefore, they were hollow and not a plating over carved figures, as were Solomon's (1 Kings 6:35). They were doubtless in several pieces, put together like those of the Candelabrum. The figures themselves were fastened to the lid in like manner (Exod. 25:19, "of the Mercy Seat," lit. *out from* it, i.e., permanently a part of it). None of the Hebrew etymologies proposed for the word *cherub* is at all satisfactory. The surmise that it may be a transposition for *rekeb,* (a *vehicle,* namely, for Jehovah), is the only one in the least degree plausible. Nor do the cognate Shemitic languages throw any light upon the derivation. Probably it is of foreign origin, perhaps Egyptian.

In shape the cherubim were substantially human, but had the split foot of an ox. The "straight foot" of Ezekiel 1:7, means the

Fig. 26.—Cherubim of an Egyptian shrine carried in a boat by priests

straight or fore leg. The same verse informs us that their color (not of the legs only) was that of polished copper. In addition to the man's face (the proper front) they had three others, namely, those of a lion and an ox, on the right and left sides, respectively, and that of an eagle behind. Again, in addition to human hands, they had two sets of wings, one pair always folded for the sake of modesty obliquely downward and forward about the person, and the other used for flight or for various expressive motions or conditions. The description in Ezekiel 1:5-14, where they are called *animals* (*chayóth,* A.V. "living creatures," like the *zoä* of the Apocalypse, A.V. unfortunately "beasts," totally different from the *cheváh,* of Dan. 7, the *theria* of Rev. 13, which are *wild* beasts, a symbol of heathen political power, like those of the Assyrian monuments), is very particular, especially verses 11 and 12, which run literally: "And their faces and their wings [were] parted from as to upward; two [of the latter as appears from v. 9] joining, each to each, and two covering their bodies. And each toward the surface of his face they went; toward withersoever the [i.e., their] spirit might be to go they went; they would not turn themselves about in going." In other words, these singular creatures had four faces and four wings apiece (but not four heads nor four bodies). Both the faces and the wings were separated at the top of the compound person into two sets of two each; the upper two of the wings extending horizontally so as to touch those of the adjoining creatures (in the form of a hollow square), and the lower two bent diagonally toward each other over the middle of the person. As they had four fronts facing in every direction, and all actuated by a common impulse, they did not need to turn round in walking or flying; but moved immediately in the direction of the face fronting the desired way. In Isaiah 6:2-7, similar figures are called *seraphim* (i.e., *burning* ones, from their flame-colored bodies), having six wings (as in Rev. 4:7, 8), four appropriated to purposes of modesty, the upper ones for veiling the face, and the lower the secret parts. We will have occasion to refer to this passage of Ezekiel more minutely hereafter.

The Cherubim were no doubt the normal or full height of a man (i.e., six feet, somewhat less than four cubits), and are always spoken of as maintaining an upright position (2 Chron. 3:13). They differ in this respect from those of the Egyptian monuments, where they are sometimes kneeling, and the Revelation, where they are often horizontal in worship. In the specimens embroidered upon the side curtains we have supposed the upper or posterior pair of wings to be folded at the back and at the sides, in a quiescent state, while those figured upon the Veil were with these wings expanded horizontally. Those upon the Ark had the same pair of wings spread obliquely upward and forward in a hovering or brooding attitude (Exod. 25:20, lit. "And the cherubs shall be [permanently] expanding [like a bird fluttering over its nest, Deut. 32:11] their wings as to upward, surrounding with their wings over the cover").[79] They stood facing each other and looking down upon the Ark. The symbolism of these postures we leave for the present, pausing here only to note that these last were on a level, one cubit from the ground, with those on the Veil, both being in a flying state, and at the same time they agreed with those on the curtains as resting upon something.

The Law

The sacred Ark contained four articles, the first and most important of which was that from which it derived its distinctive epithet, "Ark of the Covenant" (or "Ark of the Law"), namely, of God with His people. They were the two tables of stone, on which Jehovah wrote the Decalogue with His own finger, after they had been prepared by Moses to replace the original two prepared by God Himself, but broken by Moses in consequence of the idolatry of the "golden calf" (Exod. 31:18—34:29, Deut. 9:10—10:5). The only accessible stone in the immediate vicinity of Mount Sinai is the bright red granite of Jebel Mûsa itself, which is cracked into layers and checks as if by fire, or the dark porphyry of the adjoining mountains. On the summit of Jebel Mûsa there is a thin layer of compact gray granite, which might have been used. In any case two slabs of this size, one under each arm, would have been a sufficient

---

79. This whole scene is aptly illustrated by the delineations of similar figures on the monuments of Egypt (see Wilkinson's *Ancient Egyptians,* i, 267-271), as well of Assyria (Layard, *Babylon and Nineveh,* p. 643). Any objection to such representations, as conflicting with the second commandment, is obviated by the reflection that these were not figures of any actual being or creature, but only of imaginary objects.

load for a vigorous man to carry even down hill. We offer below some estimates on this point.

The second article contained in the Ark was the autograph copy of the Law, written out by Moses and deposited there (Deut. 31:26). It is presumed to be the Pentateuch in full, and thought to be the same afterwards discovered in the time of Josiah (2 Kings 22:8). This had probably been removed, together with all the contents, for in the days of Solomon the Ark contained the two tables of the Law only (1 Kings 8:9). This difficulty is discussed with great erudition and at large by A. Sennert[80], in his essay on the contents of the sacred Ark, who reaches the conclusion that all the articles enumerated were originally placed either *in* or *near* the holy receptacle. He rejects the rabbinic opinion that a different ark is also spoken of, in which the broken tables of the original copy of the Law were deposited together with these additional relics; but he is unable to determine where or by whom the latter were eventually abstracted.

The other articles deposited there were, as we learn also from Hebrews 9:4, a golden pot of the providential manna (Exod. 16:33,34), and the miraculously fruitful rod of Aaron (Num. 17:10).

Some curious calculations may be indulged in respecting the suitableness of the dimensions of the Ark for these purposes. As it was originally constructed mainly for their reception and preservation, it may be presumed to have been just large enough in length and breadth to hold them conveniently. Nevertheless, as they were comparatively thin, the box was made of shapely height, and thus there would be ample room above them for the other deposits.

Let us descend to a more minute comparison. These stone slabs were inscribed on both sides. One contained, it is generally believed, the first five commandments (all of which relate to duties towards superiors [whether God, 1-4; or parents, 5], while the other slab contained the remaining five (all of which relate to duties towards equals). Thus this corresponded very closely to our Lord's epitome of them into two precepts. The Ark had an interior capacity (if we have rightly estimated the thickness of its bottom and sides as being the same as in the case of the Table of Shewbread and the Altar of

---

80. Sennert, A., *De iis quae fuerunt in Arca Foederis,* Wittenberg, 1680.

Incense, namely $\frac{1}{12}$ of a cubit) of $2\frac{1}{2}$ cubits long, $1\frac{1}{2}$ wide, and $1\frac{5}{12}$ deep. This would allow the "Tables of the Law" to be each $2\frac{1}{2}$ cubits long, $1\frac{1}{6}$ wide, allowing $\frac{1}{6}$ of a cubit at the side for introducing the fingers in order to handle them, but giving no other play for sliding in transportation. These proportions, exactly two to one, suggest a transverse division, rather than the conventional one of a longitudinal, of each face of either slab, yielding two columns, both exact squares, for inscription. Deducting one-sixth of a cubit for margin, we have left eight spaces, each precisely one cubit square, for engraving the only words ever known to have been directly written by the Almighty in human characters. Presuming these to have been identical with those preserved to us in the two copies of the Ten Commandments (although the passages recording them, Exod. 20:2-17 and Deut. 5:6-21, have some verbal variations, with regard to which we may presume that the former is the more exact transcript), we may proceed to distribute them according to the above scheme. With Masoretic nicety we have counted the whole number of Hebrew letters in each edition (so to speak) of the Decalogue in the original. We find them to be as in the following table, including

Exodus 20			*Deuteronomy 5*		
Commandment	Verse	Letters	Commandment	Verse	Letters
	2	41		6	40
I	3	23	I	7	24
II	4	59	II	8	58
	5	74		9	74
	6	29		10	29
III	7	51	III	11	51
IV	8	18	IV	12	34
	9	24		13	24
	10	74		14	108
	11	87		15	87
V	12	53	V	16	78
VI	13	6	VI	17	6
VII	14	6	VII	18	7
VIII	15	6	VIII	19	7
IX	16	15	IX	20	16
X	17	54	X	21	60

the remarkable variation in the reason assigned for observing the Sabbath, and giving the notation of verses as in the English Bible, also the several commandments.

From this it appears that the first table of five commandments (including the prefatory verse) would contain 533 letters in Exodus (or 607 in Deuteronomy), and the second tablet only 87 in Exodus (or 96 in Deuteronomy). This is so enormous a disparity as to overthrow this logical division altogether, so far as any recognition in the original form of the Decalogue is concerned. (Judging from the most ancient MSS. and still older inscriptions, scholars are generally agreed that words were universally written without any spaces between them until comparatively recent times.)

The only equable division, unless extensive gaps or vacant spaces are admitted—a very unlikely supposition, would seem to be to put the commandments concerning the Sabbath and parents (which are quite as much a civil and human as a divine and religious statute) into the second table. So adding together the letters for command-ments 1, 2, 3 and 5 for the first tablet we find in Exodus 330 and in Deuteronomy 354. The second tablet would then contain com-mandments 4, 6, 7, 8, 9 and 10 with 290 letters in Exodus and 360 in Deuteronomy. The disparity is logical if one allows there would be blank spaces after four of the last five short commandments.

Now a single slab of ordinary marble, of the size indicated above (let us say, for convenience of comparison and calculation, four feet long by two wide), if merely *one inch* thick, would weigh about one hundred eighteen pounds, as we have computed from actually weighing a smaller piece. The tables of the law certainly could not have been thinner than this, for they would have broken by their own weight in transportation. The stone was probably not of less specific gravity than marble. At this minimum estimate, it would have been quite impossible for one person to carry two such up a steep and lofty hill, as Moses did the second pair of tablets, nor could he have clasped one of such dimensions under either arm. It is evident, therefore, that they were of but half that size, and thus intended to fit into the Ark side by side, or rather end to end. This will reduce each to a square of about $1\frac{1}{6}$ cubits, after deducting sufficient space along the sides for inserting the fingers to lift the tables when necessary, and we will leave a clear center or page for the inscription exactly one cubit square, besides a suitable margin.

Finally, it may be interesting to note that if this interior square were covered evenly by the lettering, there would be an average room of more than a square inch for each letter or, as most letters are more or less narrower than a square, it would accommodate characters about an inch long, and leave an ample blank or interval between the lines. We may, therefore, suppose that the words were arranged in ten lines with about fifteen to twenty letters to the line; distributed probably in paragraphs corresponding to the several commandments, and perhaps leaving some of the lines short, where the letters in a clause were fewer or smaller than the average.

Perfume

As accessories to the sacred apparatus, we may appropriately mention in this connection the perfumery used for this purpose exclusively, minute directions for preparing which are given. This was of two kinds, one a solid, the other a liquid.

The incense,[81] burned as we have seen above, was made of equal parts of four kinds of powerful spices, all of them except one being vegetable gums, namely, storax,[82] onycha,[83] galbanum,[84] and unadulterated frankincense,[85] triturated together to a powder (Exod. 30:34-36). Some Jewish writers add to these ingredients certain proportions of myrrh, cassia, spikenard, saffron and salt, and also

---

81. Hebrew *ketóreth has-sammím*, lit. *incense of the aromas* (A.V. "sweet incense"), i.e., perfumed, in order to distinguish it from ordinary fumigation.

82. Hebrew *natáph* (A.V. "stacte"), lit. *ooze*, i.e., distilling like drops, a resin; in this case the product of the *styrax officinale*, a small tree of Syria.

83. Hebrew *shechéleth*, lit. a *scale* (like a finger nail); the shell of the perfumed mollusk, *blatta byzantina*, found in the Mediterranean, and yielding a musky odor when burned.

84. Hebrew *chelbenáh*, lit. something *fat*, an exudation from several Oriental plants.

85. Hebrew *lebonáh*, lit. something *white;* the produce of some species of *boswellia*, grown in Arabia and Judea.

state that it was manufactured in quantities of 368 *manehs* (about 825 pounds) in a particular room of the Temple by a family of the Levites delegated for that purpose. The incense was burned twice a day (i.e., at the time of morning and evening sacrifice) on the Altar of Incense by three priests (in a later age, as we learn from Talmudic writers; but doubtless in a similar manner to the same act performed once a year by the high priest alone upon the Mercy Seat, Lev. 16:11, 12), one of whom took away the golden fire-pan and ashes of the preceding offering, another brought in a fresh pan of live coals from the great Altar, while the third performed the fuming by throwing upon the coals successive pinches of the incense, of which he carried a double fistful in the hollow of his left hand. The dense mass of smoke, which so highly volatile a substance as the incense was would immediately create, was readily carried off by the open gables of the front room and the vent at the top of the gable of the rear room.

The ointment,[86] employed in the consecration of the Tabernacle and its priests (and eventually in the inauguration of kings also), was composed of spontaneously-flowing myrrh and cassia, 500 shekels (about 680 pounds) each, and of cinnamon and calamus, half as much each, with one *hin* (about 4 quarts) of olive oil, carefully compounded into a paste (Exod. 30:23-25).

THE PRIESTS' CLOTHING

The dress of the sacerdotal order, when on duty in the sacred precincts, was minutely prescribed (Exod. 28);[87] but as no shoes or sandals are mentioned, it may be inferred that the ministrants all went barefoot, notwithstanding the exposure in inclement weather. This is confirmed by the command of Jehovah to Moses on the first

---

86. Exodus 30:25: "And thou shalt make it an oil of anointing of sanctity, a perfuming perfume, the work of a perfumer: an oil of anointing of sanctity it shall be."

87. The directions, as usual in the sacred narrative, begin with the central object, which is here the inspired ephod; but convenience with us requires the opposite order.

interview in this region, to divest himself of foot covering in the Divine Presence (Exod. 3:5).

The Levites, as being unconsecrated individually, had no canonical robes appointed for them. Therefore, they wore the dress usual with male Orientals to the present day. This substantially consists of the following pieces, omitting the *sandals* for the feet, for the reason assigned above.

First, there is a nether garment or *shirt*, usually without sleeves, loose and flowing nearly to the knees. It was of white linen (now-a-days cotton, often colored), and this is commonly the only clothing, when the wearer is at hard work. To appear elsewhere in such a state of dress was accounted as virtually being naked. (See Fig. 30.) In the case of the Levites we may suppose that it was somewhat improved beyond the lowest type. Still it doubtless consisted (substantially like the drawers described below, but folded vertically) of a simple piece of cloth about one yard wide and two yards long, doubled at the top (where a slit is made for the neck), and stitched together at the sides, except an opening at their top for the arms, the latter being covered halfway to the elbows by the loose folds at the corners. This garment is held close to the body in the middle by a *girdle,* an essential article of apparel, which served to form a pocket

Fig. 27.—A *Fellah* peasant

Fig. 28.—A *Bedouin* sheik

in the bosom and for tucking in the ends of the skirts when running, etc. (See Fig. 31.) Next comes, with all well-dressed people, an upper garment or *mantle,* frequently among the poor consisting only of a simple piece of cloth (linen or wool, colored or plain, according to circumstances), thrown loosely around the shoulders like a shawl, and hanging down nearly to the feet. In a more respectable society it frequently assumed the form of a gown, with sleeves, especially when in public with no other garment. Besides these is a *turban,* or square piece of thin cloth (linen in those days, of course), folded diagonally, and wound skillfully about the head, the ends being tucked in (see Fig. 33). Lastly, a *cloak* for rough weather, consisting of a long, thick woollen shawl, with a hole for the neck, and wrapped close about the entire body. On holiday or particular occasions, these would be exchanged for new, clean and bright garments of the same kind, or among the upper classes for other more elaborate ones, accompanied by ornaments, chiefly in the form of jewelry, such as anklets, bracelets, etc. Even men in the East do not disdain such finery. We may presume that the Levites, like other laymen, were decked with something of this higher style while ministering ("in the beauty of holiness," lit. *in the ornament of sanctity,* i.e., in festive attire, 1 Chron. 16:29; 2 Chron. 20:21; Ps. 29:2; 96:9). The drawings, from photographs of natives of the desert (Figs. 27, 28), are probably fair representations of the common outdoor garb of secular Hebrews, of the upper and lower classes respectively, at the period of the Exodus.

For all priests, however, a peculiar costume or "uniform" was imperatively ordered, while they were officially serving at the Sanctuary, although, of course, on other occasions and elsewhere they wore the ordinary dress of plain citizens. It is described in Exodus 28:40-43 and 29:8, 9, as consisting substantially of four articles, in which we may easily recognize the most essential of the above Oriental elements of apparel, with one additional note. This appears to be all that ordinary priests were to wear, while the high Priest was to have the same with certain peculiarities and additions. In the case of common priests it served as a distinction from laical apparel and also from the Levitical, by being of a more ornamental style (A.V. lit. "for glory and for beauty," the latter word being the same which we have above translated "ornament," but here enhanced by a stronger term prefixed as an adjective, i.e., "an honorary ornament" or official badge).

The Drawers or Trousers

First was a pair of linen *drawers*[88] worn for the sake of decency (as is expressly stated). These, we understand, were not in the Occidental form of trousers, but the outer covering for a modern Oriental dragoman or other elegant person, consisting merely of a

Fig. 29.—Oriental drawers for a gentleman   Fig. 30.—Oriental shirt

single piece of linen cloth, but thin and of natural color. In the case of ordinary priests, they were about a yard wide and two yards long, doubled transversely into a square bag, and stitched together at one side and at the bottom. With the selvedge top open so as to be drawn together by a cord around the waist, and a hole left in each

---

88. Hebrew only in the dual *miknesáyim,* lit. *double wrappers* (A.V. "breeches"), used only of this article, which appears to have been devised for the purpose; for Oriental nomads as well as peasants are proverbially *sans-culottes.* They reached "from the loins and as far as the thighs," which must mean that they entirely covered both these parts; i.e., they went to the knee and necessarily enough below this to fasten securely and comfortably. The legs, like the feet, were doubtless bare.

bottom corner for the legs, they could be gathered by a similar cord at the upper part of the calf like a garter. (See Fig. 29.) It is loose and cool, and though somewhat clumsy (as the width hangs in folds between the legs, and stretches out in walking), yet not ungraceful, presenting a decent medium between frock skirts and pantaloons. Common people, who otherwise go entirely naked while at work in the open fields, especially in the sultry climate of Egypt, wear, in lieu of this, a simple loin-cloth.[89]

The Tunic

Next came the *tunic*[90] either of unbleached linen or of wool, according to weather (plain for the ordinary priest), not long, for it was no doubt tucked into the drawers, like a shirt, and with sleeves, although none are alluded to in the Scriptures, and the statements of Josephus and the Rabbins are too late for this period, being evidently the common Oriental undress of the present day as above. (See Fig. 30.)

The Sash

At the middle, where these two articles met, and covering their union, was the *sash*[91] consisting of a broad band of woolen cloth,

---

89. The description of Oriental dress in Lane's *Modern Egyptians,* i, 39, is minute, but too elaborate to suit the Israelites, being largely affected by Turkish and European associations. The same is true likewise of most modern descriptions of the costumes of Syria and Asia Minor. The ancient Hebrew dress, especially of the period of the Exodus, more nearly approached the present Bedouin type, which has never materially changed. The specimen in Song of Solomon 5:11-15, is of course an unusual or wedding suit. The extreme simplicity of the principal Oriental garments makes them fit almost any person indifferently (Judg. 14:19; Matt. 22:11).

90. Hebrew *kethóneth,* lit. a *coverer,* A.V. "coat," always the garment next to the skin; as in Gen. 3:21. When it reached to the ankles, like a gown, it was properly distinguished by the epithet *passím* (lit. of the *steps,* i.e., feet, A.V. "of many [divers] colors," Gen. 37:3; 2 Sam. 13:18). The male dress of Orientals is much shorter than that of Occidentals. We must be constantly on our guard against copying European fashions in our representations of this subject. Facility of motion was the main requisite with the ancients in this matter, and even partial nudity was of little account, especially in ordinary avocations.

91. Hebrew *abnét,* lit. a *band* (A.V. "girdle"), a foreign word, used only of this

usually of bright color. In the case of an ordinary priest, to be different it is most likely at least two yards long, wound into a girdle about the waist, and tied together in front, the ends hanging down like tassels. (See Fig. 31.) The high priest's sash was quite different.

Fig. 31.—Oriental girdle (extended)

The Cap

Surmounting the figure, and completing the sacerdotal apparel, was the *cap* (the material again not prescribed), for which a different term[92] is employed respecting ordinary priests from that used in the case of the high priest. In the absence of all distinctive details, we are left to the mere etymological force of the word, aided somewhat by the customs of ancient and modern Orientals. Therefore, we hazard the conjecture that the common priestly headcovering was simply the skull-cap, which is now worn by Syrian Mohammedans night and day (being frequently changed, of course), as they generally shave the head. The Hebrews, however, appear to have kept their full hair, and to have dispensed with any headdress in ordinary avocations. (See Fig. 32.) We presume, however, that when greatly exposed out-of-doors, they wore something corresponding to the Bedouin *kefîyeh* for men, and the *veil* for women. Both of these are nothing but a square piece of cloth cast over the head and hanging down over the shoulders, the men usually fancying gay colors, and

Fig. 32—Oriental skullcap
(From a Syrian specimen)

---

priestly article, and thence transferred to the girdle of a man of rank (Isa. 22:21). It was, therefore, not the common belt (Heb. *chagór*, a *binder*, fem. *chagoráh*, which is the term usually rendered "girdle" in the A.V.).

92. Hebrew *mibgëáh*, lit. something *arched*, A.V. "bonnet."

holding theirs on by a cord around the head. (See Fig. 28.) If we are correct, the priestly cap was made up to fit the head, and of this we shall find some confirmation when we come to consider the high priest's headdress.

We will accordingly discuss the *pontifical regalia* in the same order, noting first the fact that all the articles above elucidated are present in some form or other in the high priest's attire, likewise, the trousers, shirt and cap remaining unchanged, except as to color and thickness of fabric. In Exodus 39:27-29, the shirts and caps are said to be of bleached linen, and the trousers of double-twisted material of the same sort, "for Aaron and his sons." From the fact that, in the same list, several articles are enumerated which were assigned to the high priest alone, it would appear that the addition "and his sons" there designates only the prospective high priests (as in 28:4), and not ordinary priests, for whom accordingly these pieces of clothing are elsewhere (28:40-43) specified as being of "linen" simply, i.e., thin unbleached stuff. The tunic is said to be checkered,[93] i.e., laid off in regular blocks by stripes of threads of thicker (double stranded) and bleached linen both in the warp and the woof at regular intervals among the thinner (single stranded) threads of the bleached linen foundation (for it was all still one color and material), like the "plaid muslin" of the present day. The sash was embroidered with needlework, of fancy pattern, we presume, probably uniform, because no figure is mentioned, and, if a regular one, it would be distorted by the folds and the knot. The cap is exchanged

---

93. Hebrew in the intensive conjugation, *shibbéts,* to *interweave* (A.V. "embroider"), which is used only here and of the square reticulated setting of a gem (Exod. 28:20), besides the derivative noun *tashbéts* (A.V. "broidered"), applied likewise to this tunic only (Exod. 28:4). The material is explicitly represented as to consist wholly of *bleached* stuff ("fine linen," v. 39), in distinction from the natural color of the *unbleached* flax (simple "linen," v. 42) of the trousers. The art of weaving in "diaper pattern," which is a square checker, or in "damask pattern," which is figured, but both without a change of material or color, the former being white, and the latter crimson, can hardly have been known at this early date or employed under the circumstances, as it requires an extra or *twilled* process running diagonally. The crossing of bands or stripes wider than one or two of the heavy corded threads of the "twined" or double-stranded linen would have made an uncomfortable ridge.

for a regular turban,[94] which, although likewise of plain white linen, was thus distinguished from the simpler headdress of the ordinary priest. (See Fig. 33.) Josephus' account of the high priest's dress

Fig. 33.—Oriental turban (folded)

may possibly represent with some degree of accuracy the fantastic fashions of his own age. The tiara is especially ornamental; yet it does not wholly disguise the simpler form of earlier times as we have already explained. Its triple form is probably due to the addition of the diadem by the Asmonaeans as princes, like the papal crown.

The Headgear

A notable addition to this pontifical *headgear* was a gold tablet[95] tied with a violet string,[96] doubtless by passing it through a hole at each end around the head, displaying on the front the engraved motto, in the old Hebrew characters, SANCTITY TO JEHOVAH, i.e., consecrated to His exclusive service. As the early Jewish writers are not agreed upon the width of this golden plate, nor whether the inscription was in one line or two, we have consulted the proprieties of the case, and the good taste of the majority of archaeologists, in the matter. Josephus states that the pontifical frontlet made by Solomon was in existence in his own day.[97] In that case it was probably among the spoils of Jerusalem exhibited at the triumph of Titus, and finally deposited in the temple of Peace at Rome.[98] Origen, however, asserts that it was the original one of Aaron, and

---

94. Hebrew *mitsnépheth,* a *coiling* (A.V. "mitre"), used only for this pontifical article, and once (Ezek. 21:26) for the "diadem" of a prince; the simpler form *tsaníph* being employed indiscriminately ("mitre," Zech. 3:5; "diadem," Job 29:14; Isa. 62:3; "hood," Isa. 3:23), and the corresponding verb *tsanáph,* applied to convolutions (Isa. 22:18), as well as to this piece of attire (Lev. 16:4). We have avoided all unnecessary complications.

95. Hebrew *tsits,* lit. a *glitter,* i.e., a "plate," or narrow thin strip.

96. Hebrew *pethíl,* lit. *twist,* a *thread* (A.V. "lace").

97. Josephus, *Antiquities of the Jews,* VIII, iii, 6.

98. Josephus, *Wars of the Jews,* VII, v, 7.

that it remained till his time. Also it was inscribed with Samaritan characters, by which, of course, he means the antique Hebrew.[99]

The Robe

Proceeding to the vestments altogether peculiar to the pontiff, as compared with his subalterns, we have a *robe,*[100] which was but another tunic, of simpler pattern and without sleeves. Being of the form which we have described above as that of an ordinary Oriental shirt, the selvedge was merely stitched together for sides, with openings for the arms. The hole in the fold at the top bound (like a coat of mail, A.V.), had an edge woven on in making, to prevent its ravelling or tearing. The text is very explicit (Exod. 28:31, 32), literally:"And thou shalt make a robe of the ephod, wholly violet; and there shall be a mouth [i.e. hole] of its head [i.e. top] in its middle: a lip [i.e. selvedge or woven edge] there shall be to its mouth around: the work of a weaver, like the mouth of a corslet, there shall be to it: it shall not be torn." In other words, it was to be a single piece of cloth, with an opening for the neck made in the weaving. This could only be effected, in the simple loom of those days, by parting the threads, both of the warp and the woof, around a cylinder inserted for that purpose, and holding them in place by double overcast stitches crossing each other in opposite directions. It was not to be cut, but of course had a hemmed bottom (v. 33), and a seam at the side, with a space left open as an armhole. The seamless "coat" of later times (John 19:23) was a *tunic.*

The robe was to be wholly of violet, hence wool both warp and woof. It was probably long enough to reach about to the knee. The bottom hem was decorated with a fringe consisting of alternate little bells of gold (probably a globe with a ball within it, like sleigh bells) and artificial pomegranates (i.e., globular tassels) of woolen threads (tufted, as we presume,) of the three sacred colors, violet, purple and crimson (not mixed, we suppose, but one of each in

---

99. Josephus, *Antiquities of the Jews,* III, vii, 6, Whiston's note.

100. Hebrew *mëïl,* lit. an *upper* (i.e. outer) garment, spoken of any such piece of clothing in general use, sometimes "mantle" in the A.V.

regular succession, like the bands on the curtains). The bells were designed for giving notice of the functionary's approach so that no impure person or thing might meet him, and thus, however inadvertently or unconsciously to him, expose him to divine visitation for entering upon his duties in that condition. The woolen balls were for variety. As their number is not given, we may conjecturally hang them by a golden wire or yellow silk cord one-sixth of a cubit apart, making perhaps twelve bells and as many tassels, four of each color. The rabbinical statements concerning the seventy-two bells on the high priest's robe, and that it was woven seamless[101] relate to customs introduced at a later age than that of which we treat. It does not follow from the allusions in Revelation 1:13 and 16:6, that the pontifical girdle was but a little below the armpits, for in that case the bottom of the breastplate could not have been fastened to it; any more than that the robe reached to the feet, as it clearly did not.[102] These last two features, in the case of an active official, would have been effeminate, disproportioned and inconvenient. They are borrowed from the description of Josephus,[103] but are not countenanced by the language of the sacred text, as belonging to the original attire of the high priest.

The Ephod

Immediately over this article of dress (hence called "the robe of the ephod") was placed the principal token of the high priest's rank, called the *ephod* (its Heb. name, signifying a *girdle,* but not the common word for that piece of apparel). This was made of the same stuff as the Veil, tricolor woollen bands on a white double-stranded linen ground, embroidered with figures in gold (thin plates cut into narrow strips and used as thread, Exod. 39:13). It consisted of two

101. Edersheim, *The Temple and its Services,* pp. 72-73.

102. *loc. cit.*

103. Josephus, *Antiquities of the Jews,* III, vii, 2.

Fig. 34.—Ancient Egyptian chief priest (with apron-like drawers, leopard-skin ephod, tankard for libation, and censer)

Fig. 35.—The Ephod extended

shoulder-pieces,[104] sewed together by the raw edges in a seam.[105] Each was about one cubit wide by one and one-half long, hanging by the neck (where a hole, of course, was made and bound), one over the bosom, and the other over the back, down to the waist. These were fastened, doubtless at the bottom, by a belting-strap[106] (one, of course, on each side), made of the same materials as the ephod itself (the ends tied together in a bow-knot at the hip). At the

104. Hebrew sing. *kathéph,* lit. a *lateral* projection, designating the *top* or ridge of the shoulder, in distinction from the back part or shoulder blade, for which a different word is employed.

105. The Hebrew terms are the same as those which we have shown, in discussing the Tabernacle curtains, to be carefully used in these senses. The ephod was not a single piece, like the robe over which it was worn, but made to be joined together at the top (the open sides were of course the straight selvedge), because that part had to be nicely fitted to the slope of the shoulders, as it was to sustain several appendages.

106. Hebrew *chésed appudathó,* lit. "strap of its belting," the latter term being from the same root as *ephod.*

top seam, in the middle of the shoulder slope, were sewed on two studs, one on each side, consisting each of onyx,[107] large enough (perhaps $\frac{1}{12}$ of a cubit square) to contain the engraved letters of six of the names of the twelve sons of Israel, beginning probably with that on the right shoulder, and arranged, we may suppose, from analogy of the loaves of shewbread, in a single column. The longest of these names (we suppose them here to be set down in the actual order of birth, namely, Reuben, Simeon, Levi, Judah, Dan, Naphtali, Gad, Issachar, Asher, Zebulon, Joseph, Benjamin), is in the Hebrew *Benjamin,* which has six letters (showing that our arrangement would produce a square). If the names were displayed separately and not run together, as often in old MSS. and inscriptions, our estimate would allow each letter a space of $\frac{1}{12}$ of a cubit (about $\frac{1}{3}$ of an inch). The stone was set in a reticulated gold plate[108] sewed by the interstices on the garment, to which was attached a twisted gold chain (lit. *links . . . wreathed . . . cords,* A.V. "chains . . . at the ends . . . wreathen"), for fastening it to the pectoral, as presently explained.

The Pectoral

The *pectoral,* which was the crowning glory of the high priest's regalia, and the most sacred talisman of his office, is styled a *spangle*

---

107. Hebrew *shóham,* of obscure derivation, and designating some kind of gem, but certainly not the *diamond,* for that cannot be engraved, and is too small and costly. It was the same as the eleventh stone in the breastplate.

108. Hebrew *mishbétseth,* a *texture* by embroidery (Ps. 45:13, "wrought"), hence a netted socket for a gem. The Hebrew term here used for the mode of insertion, *musabbóth* (A.V. "set in," "enclosed in"), although originally the feminine plural of a passive participle meaning *turned about,* is constantly used as a noun, in the sense of *reversal.* Therefore, it always stands before the word which it qualifies in the construction, and not after it as an adjective would. Accordingly, we must here render, "Reverses of settings of gold shalt thou make them;" and in Exodus 39:6, "reverses of settings of gold," and in 39:13, "reverses of settings of gold in their bezels." In like manner, at Ezekiel 41:24 (A.V., "two turning leaves"), we must render "two folds of leaves;" and in the sole remaining occurrence of the word (Num. 32:38, A.V., "their names being changed"), no other rendering is grammatically possible than parenthetically "transmutations of names."

(from its sparkling gold and flashing gems).[109] It was substantially a bag of the same materials as the ephod itself, one span (or half a cubit, i.e., about ten inches) square, when folded at the bottom, and sewed together at the sides. The face (or outer layer) had on it (apparently stitched on like studs, at regular intervals, but probably very close together, so as to bend to fit the person) gold plates, doubtless of the same general style as those on the shoulders, in which were set precious stones, in four rows, engraved respectively with the names of the twelve tribes of Israel. We presume the names were in the conventional order of encampment (in which the same division of 4×3 occurs), as in the following diagram, doubtless three columns of four names each, as symmetry of space requires, and as a "row" in reading would mean (but not elsewhere). As there was

3. Zebulon	2. Issachar	1. Judah
6. Gad	5. Simeon	4. Reuben
9. Benjamin	8. Manasseh	7. Ephraim
12. Naphtali	11. Asher	10. Dan

but one name on each stone, there would be room for letters much larger than those on the shoulder studs. The modern equivalents of few, if any of the gems, are known with certainty (comp. the similar list in Rev. 21:19, 20). The following table identifies them as nearly as may be:

---

109. Hebrew *chóshen,* lit., it would seem, for the root is found in no other word, a *glistening* (A.V. "breastplate"), used only of this particular ornament; often with the additional epithet, "of judgment," because oracular decisions were obtained by its means.

Row	Order	A.V. Rendering	Hebrew Name	Modern Name	Probable Color
I.	1.	Sardius	*ódem*	carnelian	light red
	2.	Topaz	*pitdáh*	chrysolite	bright yellow
	3.	Carbuncle	*baréketh*	emerald	grass green
II.	4.	Emerald	*nóphek*	garnet	dark red
	5.	Sapphire	*sappír*	lapis-lazuli	deep blue
	6.	Diamond	*yahalom*	chalcedony	pink
III.	7.	Ligure	*léshem*	jacinth	buff
	8.	Agate	*shebó*	agate	red streaks
	9.	Amethyst	*achlamáh*	amethyst	purplish
IV.	10.	Beryl	*tarshísh*	topaz	dull yellow
	11.	Onyx	*shóham*	beryl	pale green
	12.	Jasper	*yashephéth*	jasper	clouded gray

The entire "breastplate" was held upon the ephod by fastenings that are minutely and somewhat intricately described. In Exodus 28:22-28 it will be observed by the reader, that we have three terms carefully applied to the different aspects of a piece of cloth, precisely in accordance with the significance that we have previously pointed out, although they are confused in the A.V.: *éber* is the *surface* (as of the tables of the Law), *sapháh* is the free *selvedge,* and *katsáh* is a hemmed (or at least seamed) end. The other expressions in this description are also as before explained. For the sake of clearness we literally translate the whole of the last paragraph, with explanatory interpolations in brackets:

V. 22. "And thou shalt make upon the breastplate wreathed chains [i.e., links twisted or bent so as to lie all flat], the work of cords [i.e., links of round wire], pure gold."

V. 23. "And thou shalt make upon the breastplate two rings of gold; and thou shalt put the two rings upon the two ends [*katsáh* (i.e., upper or hemmed edge)] of the breastplate."

V. 24. "And thou shalt put the two cords [i.e., chains] of gold upon the two rings towards the ends [*katsáh*] of the breastplate."

V. 25. "And the two [other] ends [*katsáh* (i.e., the end-links destitute of a hook)] of the two cords [i.e., gold chains (namely, those previously mentioned, v. 14)] thou shalt put upon the two intertextures [i.e., reticulated settings], and [thus] thou shalt put [them] upon the shoulders [i.e., sides] of the ephod, towards the front of its face [(the same expression as used concerning the gable overlap of the roof canvas), i.e., across its very face]."

V. 26. "And thou shalt make two [other] rings of gold, and thou shalt put them upon the two ends [*katsáh* (i.e., lower, but still seamed edges, because the two selvedges are there sewed together)] of the breastplate, upon its selvedges [*sapháh,* i.e., still such, although double], which [are] towards the surface [*éber*] of the ephod inward [i.e., lie close upon the ephod beneath, and never rise from it, as do the upper corners, when the mouth of the sack is opened]."

V. 27. "And thou shalt [also] make two [corresponding] rings of gold, and thou shalt put them upon the two shoulders [i.e., sides] of the ephod, from as to downward [i.e., near the bottom], from the front of its face [i.e., on its very face], to the conjunctions of [i.e., opposite] its joining [by stitches to the strap], from above as to [i.e., near the top of] the strap of the ephod."

V. 28. "And they [i.e., the makers or weavers] shall tie the breastplate from [i.e., by] its [lower] rings towards [i.e., to] the rings of the ephod with a thread of violet [wool], [so as] to be upon the strap of the ephod; and the breastplate shall not be shoved from upon the ephod."

We epitomize by saying that the pectoral had a gold ring in each of its four corners. The two at the top were joined to the ephod by a continuation of the twisted chains already attached to the shoulder

Fig. 36.—Twisted chain

studs (the hook being apparently, as usual in such cases, on the end of the upper chain for entering any convenient link in the lower chain). The bottom rings were tied by a violet cord to rings inserted in the ephod at the point where the straps branched off. These four fastenings (the upper ones stronger, as bearing the weight) would stretch diagonally and keep the pectoral extended and yet closed, at the middle of the breast.

The Urim and the Thummim

Finally, the sacred pocket thus suspended over the very heart of the high priest, where it would be inviolably safe, and at the same time accessible at a moment's notice, was designed—in a manner analogous (as we shall presently see more fully) to the inmost Ark of the Sanctuary—as a place of deposit for the most priceless blessing of God to His fallen, erring children, a mode of ascertaining His will. The physical instrument of this form of divine communication was the famous *Urim and Thummim,* Hebrew terms that have greatly vexed the learning and ingenuity of interpreters, with less satisfactory results, perhaps, than any other part of the whole Tabernacle apparatus. The following is a condensed summary of all the positive information that philology and the Scriptures afford on this difficult but interesting topic. Neither Josephus nor the Rabbins seem to have had access to anything further, while the conjectures of modern writers are mostly worse than worthless.

The words "the Urim and the Thummin" are not proper names. "Urim" is simply the plural of *ûr,* which is occasionally used in the singular for *light* (as is its congener *ôr* constantly) in the sense of *flame* (Isa. 31:9; 44:16; 47:14; 50:11; Ezek. 5:2; for it is merely the infinitive of the common verb meaning *to shine*), and for Ur, the birthplace of Abraham; while the plural (besides the distinctive use here considered, occurring *singly* in Num. 27:21; 1 Sam. 28:6; and elsewhere in the *compound* phrase, Exod. 28:30; Lev. 8:8; Deut. 33:8; Ezra 2:63; Neh. 7:65) is used for the region of lights, i.e., the East (Isa. 24:15, A.V. "fires"). "Thummim" likewise is only the plural form of *tôm,* meaning *perfection,* and usually rendered, in the singular, "integrity" (Gen. 20:5, 6; 1 Kings 9:4; Ps. 7:8; 25:21; 26:1, 11; 41:12; 78:72; Prov. 19:1; 20:7), "uprightness," "upright," or "uprightly" (Job 4:6; Prov. 2:7; 10:9, 29; 13:6; 28:6), "perfect" or "perfection" (Ps. 101:2; Isa. 47:9), "simplicity" (2 Sam. 15:11), "full" (Job 21:23), "at a venture" (1 Kings 22:34; 2 Chron. 18:33), but in the plural only in connection with Urim. The plural form of both words does not necessarily imply that there were many of each kind of object, nor even that the two were distinct articles; but rather according to a frequent Hebrew idiom, these peculiarities of the phrase express as follows: the plural, emphasis or quantity; and the duplication, attribution or quality. Thus a free translation would be *full* light as to amount and *perfect* as to kind, i.e., complete illumination; in modern terminology, *a definite oracle,* in distinction from the vague and ambiguous intimations from other sources, whether heathen shrines, providential auguries, or even inspired vaticinations, such as had been the only resource of previous ages and other nations.

As to the actual application of this instrumentality for predicting events, we find various significant facts. The object in question was small, light and non-fragile in order to be easily carried in the pouch of the breastplate. It (or its equivalent) was duplicated freely in the pontifical family (1 Sam. 22:18), but the acting high priest alone had the prerogative of consulting it (1 Sam. 23:2, 4, 6). The secret of using it was at length lost even to the hierarchy (Ezra 2:63). The questions put by its means were categorical, and the answers were equally explicit, although not always a simple affirmative or negative (1 Sam. 23:9-12; 2 Sam. 5:23, 24); and sometimes refused altogether (1 Sam. 28:6). All this implies a material apparatus, a public consultation, and a palpable reply, either by visible or audible signs. It excludes all theories of priestcraft, fortunetelling or legerdemain, making the whole a *bona fide* supernatural indication of what no mortal could of himself discover or predict. Beyond this everything concerning it is uncertain, and the speculations of scholars are scarcely worth recounting.

Without entering in detail into the hopeless discussion on this mysterious subject, we may safely say, in brief, that these terms designate some means of oracular response, on questions of public importance, by Jehovah through the high priest. The manner in which they are introduced ("*the* Urim and *the* Thummim," like "*the* Cherubim," on their first mention), yet without any explanation, shows that they were well known already to the Israelites. This adds force to the presumption, confirmed by an inspection of the monuments, that they were the originals of which the symbolical images, known to Egyptologists as those of the double goddess of Truth and Justice,[110] and probably also the idolatrous Teraphim of the early Mesopotamians and later Syrians, were the counterfeits. We risk the opinion that this species of augury was by means of an image (probably of clay rudely modelled) representing *truth* as the essential attribute of deity. It was worn in the bosom, which is the Oriental pocket, in order to be always at hand. Like the cherubim, its purely ideal character relieved it of the charge of idolatry. The only clue to its mode of manipulation for obtaining an oracular response is given in 1 Samuel 14:19 (for the *ephod* and not the *ark* must be there referred to; comp. v. 3, and see Keil on the passage), where the expression "withdraw [literally *"gather* up"] thy hand" shows that it was held in the open hand during consultation. It does not seem, however, to have been absolutely necessary in the process at all, for on several occasions no mention of it whatever is made (1 Sam. 23:2, 4; 2 Sam. 5:19, 23; 21:1). In one instance at least it was impliedly absent, the priestly vestment itself being only an ordinary one of simple linen, such as appears to have been worn by the whole lineage of the high priest (1 Sam. 23:6; comp. 22:18). This lends color to the suspicion that the response was not given by any peculiarity of the object in question itself; but was merely divined through some professional skill acquired by the officiator (comp. John 11:51). Finally, inasmuch as in several of the above cases even the priestly intervention is not positively stated, it may be that the king or any other public functionary was qualified to ascertain the divine will by this means.

However that may be, we find this mode of divination in use among the Hebrews from this time forward, as it appears to have been in the patriarchal days (Gen. 25:22, 23), down to a late period of the Jewish commonwealth, when it suddenly and silently disappears altogether from history. This was because it was superseded by the clearer and fuller lights and perfections of personally-inspired prophets, whose oral deliverances, afterwards compiled by themselves in permanent documents, have survived the vicissitudes of transcription and denationalization, and still guide and cheer the saints on their march to the heavenly home.

---

110. See Wilkinson, *Ancient Egyptians,* ii, 27; v. 28.

CHAPTER 3
SYMBOLISM OF THE TABERNACLE

We approach this enticing part of our study with much caution, and only after we have prepared the way for it by a careful analysis of the facts and elements upon which a figurative application of the whole or any of its correlated parts should rest. We are moreover warned, by the extravagant and unseemly mystifications of most predecessors in this attempt, how liable a fertile fancy is to mislead even a well-stored head and a well-disposed heart in a field where so little is fixed by determinative bounds, whether historical, logical, philosophical or artistic. Much that has been given by former writers as symbol on this subject is merely *metaphor* or figure of speech instead of representation by object. The symbolism of the Tabernacle, as developed briefly by Josephus and Philo, is purely *cosmical;* and in this they are followed more at length by Bähr. The barrenness and coldness of such an exposition are sufficiently obvious. Later expositors have usually vibrated between this and the merely clerical idea of the Tabernacle symbolism, or else they have gone off on some tangential line suggested by their own subjective inclinations. Such whims can neither be proved nor disproved. The competent objection to them is their inadequacy and their triviality. They mistake accidental and partial coincidence for designed and sustained correspondence. Scriptural typology must be deduced by rigid exegesis and a broad view of the divine economy, especially in its soteriological relations. This is the core of revelation. The legitimate tests of the symbolism of the Tabernacle, as of that of any Jewish or Christian institution, are natural congruity, spiritual suggestiveness, and biblical sanction. It is not enough to cover the requirements of a perfunctory ritualism, a stolid ecclesiasticism, or a conventional nationalism, much less to satisfy the most obvious demands of an outward naturalism; the deep value of a universal, sempiternal and soul-saving import must be reached. The Tabernacle was the visible hearthstone of the invisible Church, then first laid in a fixed though still (as ever on earth) migratory habitation. It was the type of that "house of God" which was designed to embrace the globe, to be the germ of heaven, and yet to dwell in the humblest heart. Its archetype, modelled in the conclave of the eternal Trinity, and for a brief season disclosed to Moses, still remains in the celestial sphere, to be unveiled at length to the full satisfaction of all the saints. There we shall forever admire the perfection of the symbol and its object.

The only safe guide, in our judgment, is direct scriptural warrant for the aesthetic analogies and spiritual symbols which this elaborate and elegant structure must have been intended to bring out. This exposition of the true aim and inner moral of such a picture-lesson to the comparatively infantile mind of the Israelites must be sought either in the explicit statements of the sacred text (whether of the Old or the New Testament), or else in the inferences naturally growing out of them, and essential in order to maintain their coherence and symmetry. We, therefore, propose, not mainly to reject, nor polemically to dissect the occult and often microscopic resemblances which most writers on the subject have debated or fancied in these gorgeous emblems, ranging through earth, air, sea and sky; but to compare, combine and deduce what strikes us as a self-disclosed and tangible system of religious truth modelled into the coincidences and varieties of this remarkable piece of handicraft. We shall find that its doctrine, no less than its composition, is organic and harmonic, especially in its most peculiar features.

In a general way, we may remark, as a preliminary thought, that the Tabernacle, as a whole, being in fact but a *tent,* is occasionally referred to in the Scriptures as a type of a *transient* sojourn. Such it was among the nomadic Israelites in the desert, while on their journey to Canaan, which was a symbol of the passage of saints through the stage of mortal probation to their heavenly home. Such it was also to Jehovah, prior to His more permanent residence in the stone structure of the Temple on the permanent site of Jerusalem. In a more special sense, it may perhaps have prefigured the occupancy of a human body by the Messiah during His stay on earth (John 1:14, render "tabernacled" instead of "dwelt;" and compare Peter's language, Matt. 17:4). It is also an apt figure of the frail abode of every one of His followers on earth (2 Peter 1:13, 14).

NUMERICAL SIGNIFICANCE

The first thing that occurs at the very threshold of our attempts at reconstruction or survey is the principle of thorough proportion that reigns throughout the mechanical execution of the Tabernacle, extending to the smallest and most secret parts. Proportion is the principle that combines unity with variety, holding the universe together, and rendering man a miniature of Deity. It is the harmony of the spheres and the symmetry of the atom. It is the algebra of beauty and the mechanics of morals. It is the prime quality of object teaching, from the hornbook to the calculus; and very properly does it stand prominent in the frontispiece of the picture lessons of the Tabernacle. It is the ground idea of the whole structure. For the Architect of Nature works always by rule, and the products of His recreation are destined eventually to exhibit no less perfection. They are to be copies on a smaller scale of His infinite proportions. This proportion appears on the face of the plan and its accompaniments in the numbers and sizes given by the architects. We will take these in their arithmetical order, gradually contracting to the central identity. They all have a natural, rather than a metaphysical basis.

The Decimal

The simplest and earliest, as well as the most scientific and perfect measure of enumeration is the decimal one, which in modern metrology threatens to supersede all others in exact or even popular specification. The ten fingers evidently suggested the digits (their namesake), and men spontaneously count by their means. In the Tabernacle all the ground plans and elevations proceed by tens or a multiple or integral part of ten. Wherever this is practicable, it is maintained in the subdivisions of space and material. This is too obvious to need illustration.

The practical lesson from this basic distribution seems to be, that the entire edifice, with its court, its rooms, its walls, its pillars, its curtains and its fastenings, was meant to be a thing of convenience as well as of regularity. Also its economy, both in construction and in use, was to be a mathematical teacher to the unschooled but acute genius of the chosen people. Even to our own day, the lesson, that "order is heaven's first law," and that the most perfect conventional exponent in numerical proportion is essential for the purpose of expressing and maintaining this order, is by no means superfluous. Indeed, it is growingly appreciated and inculcated.

It is true that the duodecimal system, as in the multiplication table, is occasionally employed in the Tabernacle, and was suggested perhaps at first by the months of the year (although this is not strictly true of the Jewish calendar, and is itself but an artificial basis for calculation). In the present case it was emphasized by the number of the sons and tribes of Israel; but this is carried no further than those few particulars that directly memorialize the ancestral and territorial sections of the nation, and have no essential root in the great features of the Tabernacle and its cultus.

Seven

The next primary[1] number, namely, the septenary, that runs throughout the dimensions, but less conspicuously, was obviously

---

1. We observe here incidentally, but significantly, that the three primary (and in Hebrew nomenclature the "sacred") numbers seven, three and one, which, like the prismatic colors, blue, red and yellow, make up the others, are all *odd,* and hence indivisible without fractions. The first two yield by addition the round ten, the second by successive self-multiplications that most peculiar of all squares nine (the magic sum of all the other digits ranged around the central five, and the

drawn from the days of the week, an Edenic distribution, for reasons which the most exact experience of modern times has vindicated as necessary for the human economy, both in the individual and in society. It comes in most opportunely to resolve the singular variation in the length of the inside curtains as compared with the roof canvas ($7 \times 4 = 28$), and especially as a basis of the two factors four and three, which enter so largely into the other dimensions. It may have been intended to serve as a reminder of the Sabbath as well as of the sacredness of an oath.

Four

The quadruple distribution, as just observed, prevails in the square horizontal forms generally adopted in the Tabernacle, as well as in many of the upright ones (the number of the doorway posts for example, and the rings at the corners of the pieces of furniture). It has its own distinctive lesson as we will presently see.

Three

The triple arrangement, as the remainder of seven, has a very marked position as a factor in the Tabernacle economy, as already noticed. Some may think the allusion to the persons of the Deity here as premature as would be a reference to the mathematical proportions of the triangle. Yet the tripartite division of the terrestrial universe (land, sea and atmosphere), as well as of its associated elements (water, fire and air), would illustrate this. Even the great kingdoms (animal, vegetable and mineral), and the forms of life (beasts, birds and fishes), including the constituents of man himself (popularly called body, soul and spirit), cannot have been altogether accidental correspondences to this architectural fact, any more than they are to the aphorism that almost everything may be as readily and, usually, more logically divided into threes as into halves.

---

instant dissolvent of all other products), while the unit, perfect in itself, neither increases nor diminishes the others by proportion. The complicated relations of involution and evolution, of course, are foreign to so primitive an arithmetic.

Two

The duplicate division, too obvious in the Tabernacle to need specification, is based upon the sexual distinction, no less than the grand distribution of "the earth and the heavens," the former again being divisible in the land and water. Its great lesson is the dualism that pervades not only nature (chiefly as opposites, e.g., heat and cold, light and darkness, but sometimes as allies, e.g., food and drink, light and heat), but still more significantly the moral realm (virtue and vice, God and Satan).

One

Finally, the single object, as the germ of all, most strikingly suggest the unity of all things, especially in God the universal Maker, Preserver and Judge, and the only being entitled to worship in any realm of existence (heaven, earth or hell).

The Cubit

The cubit itself, which is constantly the measure throughout the Tabernacle and its appurtenances, is a natural standard, being the normal length of the forearm, or the distance from the elbow to the wrist in a full-sized man (Deut. 3:11). In the figurative idiom of the Hebrew its name is characteristically *ammáh,* which is merely a variation[2] of the word *êm,* a *mother,* not so much (as the lexicons explain[3]) "because the forearm is the mother of the [entire] arm" (a metaphor not very obvious surely), but because the cubit (or *ulna*) is the "mother," as it were, of all dimensions whether in the human body[4] or elsewhere.

---

2. It is in fact the feminine form, for *êm* (a "mother" in the lit. sense), being a primitive word, actually has the masculine or root form.

3. Gesenius expressly says, "mother of the arm," citing Deut. 3:11, as authority; and Fürst substantially does the same, giving the word the original sense of "*elbow-joint,* then *arm,* and lastly more specially the *fore* or *lower arm.*"

4. In like manner tailors and mantua-makers frequently reckon the proportions of a garment by the length of a finger, or the size of the chest; and glove-fitters by the diameter of the hand or even of the wrist. In conclusion, we may compare the kindred standards of a palm, a finger-breadth, etc.

Fractions

It deserves notice that no irregular multiples or fractions are employed in the measurements of the Tabernacle, nor, with the exception of the dimensions of the Table of Shewbread and of the Ark, which are a regular aliquot part, namely the half of five and three respectively, is any *mixed* number, consisting of a whole number and a fraction, either expressed or implied. In the number twelve the essential symbolism is sought, not in the months of the year (which among the Hebrews, being lunar, were often thirteen), much less in the signs of the zodiac (which are an astronomical refinement), but in the product of the only two subdivisions possible of the number seven. "Dozen" is a modern unit arithmetically, and even in the multiplication table the decimal limit would have been more natural, and probably more convenient. This number accordingly is only employed in Scripture *conventionally,* and derives its whole significance from that of the tribes of Israel, whence it was transferred to the apostles as representatives of the Christian Church. It is, therefore, purely national and ecclesiastical.

In like manner the number seven, while having no strictly natural type, was formally adopted as the *sacred* number from the institution of the Sabbath as a holy season, and accordingly it enters conspicuously into the symbolism of the Tabernacle as an element of dimension in the enigmatic curtains only, and in the deeply significant lamps of the candelabrum.

So again the numbers three and four, components of seven and twelve by addition and multiplication respectively, are not derived from any such abstract notions as (for the former) the three divisions of the universe (air, earth and sea), dimensions of space (length, breadth and thickness), or the Trinity, nor (for the latter) the four points of the compass, etc. Rather they are the basis of the only two perfect forms (besides the circle which is the type of unity), namely the square and the triangle, of which we treat elsewhere. Accordingly, they also appear only in the *utilitarian* details of the Tabernacle, unless we except the tripartite or quadruple colors (strictly quintuple) of the sacred textures.

SYMBOLISM OF COLOR

As the next element of symbolism we place color, for that is truly the basis of form, since the shape of objects is really determined by the variations of color or the degrees of shading at the edges. Outlines differ according to the point of view or the aspect, while the color, at however great distances (if the object be distinctively visible), remains constantly the same. Indeed without color, which is but a variation of light, any object is altogether invisible. We should note that all the colors of the Tabernacle were what are called "fast," i.e., permanent, or not liable to fade. Hence none of them is drawn from the vegetable kingdom, nor used in dyeing vegetable materials.

If it be true that "order is Heaven's first law," it is equally true that proportion is Order's first law, and that number is the basis of proportion. Form or figure is ultimately resolvable into the three constituents of the number, relative dimensions and proportion of the parts, the latter two of which are also expressible only in numbers. All these are in the department of mathematics, which applies two of the senses, touch and sight, to the mutual corroboration of absolute truth. Color, on the other hand, is an independent quality, recognizable only by the latter of these senses, and residing wholly in the surface of objects, which, likewise, is the field of the former sense, while their substance is comprehended under form and number. It is certain, however, that color itself is produced by the shape of the exterior particles of the matter of bodies, for it is refracted, diffracted and reflected according to this, and the hue of substances may be changed by merely polishing or powdering them, the superficial atoms acting as minute prisms in resolving the rays.

Color, therefore, is a purely accidental or artificial quality of the outside, while those attributes that have been hitherto considered are naive and inherent to the essence of the matter. For this reason we are prepared to expect that its symbolism will be conventional in the highest degree, and we shall, accordingly, find that it enters into the sensuous imagery of the Tabernacle to express covenant relations only, addressed solely to the eye of faith, and not belonging to the natural properties of things. The three remaining senses are in their turn presented each with their appropriate fields of symbolism in the concomitant of worship, the silver trumpets for the ear, the incense for the nose, the tithes for the palate. Modern science, however, has demonstrated that all the senses are affected by undulations or pulsations upon the nervous extremities of the appropriate organ, and that colors no less than sounds, and doubtless also smells, tastes and tactual perceptions, are differentiated by arithmetical ratios in the waves and strokes through the medium. The proportions of numbers, therefore, are constantly the index of order in nature, and this is at least a hint of the method of "grace upon grace" graduated after the lesson of the parable of the pounds or the talents.

Black

We begin, therefore, with *black,* which is, strictly speaking, the absence of all color, and therefore the emblem of secrecy, mourning, etc., as darkness is of death, sin, etc. In the Tabernacle, accordingly, where cheerfulness is the prevailing idea (for the worship of Jehovah, however awful, is not to be regarded in a forbidding aspect), there is but little occasion for using this color. Even then it is in a softened phase, namely, the dusky goats'-hair canvas. Here it is taken in the amiable or benign symbolism of protection or privacy, as the roof covers and screens the dwellers from exposure to the sun and the rain, and also from the public gaze or intrusion. For a similar reason there was no artificial light in the Most High Place, as this was the secret chamber of Jehovah, illuminated regularly by His own sun alone, and occasionally by His specially revealed Shekinah. Thus He "in whom [intrinsically] there is no darkness at all" (1 John 1:5), nevertheless, under the preparatory dispensation of Judaism, "would dwell in the thick darkness" (1 Kings 8:12), until the Light of Life, "the effulgence of His glory" (Heb. 1:3), came forth from "the light that no man can approach unto" (1 Tim. 6:16), to open the secrets of His nature to man

(John 1:18), and to dissipate the gloom of sinfulness and the grave (2 Tim. 1:10).

White

As the harmonious blending of all the prismatic colors, although not reckoned as a peculiar color at all, *white* continually reappears in the Tabernacle, the opposite of black and the emblem of innocence in the scriptural sense of justification, including pardon, purity and peace. It gleams in the silvery sockets, hooks, rods, etc., emblems of the attractive points of connection between the various stages in divine worship. It is untinged in the inviting exterior of the Court, and in the clean inner garments of the pontificate.[5] It is tinted with softer hues in the entrance and side screens and in the more ornamental parts of the high priest's apparel. If, as we have conjectured, the fur of the inner skin-blanket of the walls were that of a grayish goat or antelope,[6] it will correspond well with the unbleached material of the sacerdotal drawers (of flax), cap and shirt (either of flax or wool), worn next to the person. This was not

---

5. On one occasion only, namely, the great day of annual atonement (Lev. 16:4, 23, if we are correct in understanding the "holy garments" of simple "linen," there mentioned, to have been a special suit of unbleached stuff), was this rule departed from, in order to symbolize the general sinfulness of the priesthood as well as laity, whom the high priest then impersonated, as if in weeds of half-mourning. The earthly representative was not allowed to enter Jehovah's immediate presence without a badge of his imperfect purity, but the ever-sinless High Priest ascended within the heavenly veil in His original vesture of perfect glory.

There was also a utilitarian purpose in this change of clothing, in order not to soil the pontifical regalia with the blood which the high priest was required to sprinkle so freely during this ceremony about the entire premises (vv. 14, 15, "upon the mercy seat eastward" is immediately explained by "before" the mercy seat, i.e., on the ground in front or on the east side, not on the lid of the Ark itself; so in v. 18, the "altar that is before the Lord" is the copper altar of burnt offering, not the golden altar of incense).

6. The *tachash* was, of course, a ceremonially "clean" animal, and this at once excludes all the conjectures of a marine creature, whether of the seal or porpoise tribe. Although these may possess fins, they certainly have no scales (see Lev. 11:9-12; Deut. 14:9, 10). It was probably of the goat or antelope genus, several specimens of which of a suitable character are found in the adjacent regions, and

so dazzling white as to show the slight discoloration of necessary wear, but yet white enough to betray any real soil or foreign substance. This may have hinted at the everyday hue of practical piety in this work-a-day world, not too nice for mortal touch, and yet not stained by actual sin; while the unsullied lustre of the bleached linen on the outmost enclosure, and on the body and head of the high priest, was a type of the immaculate pale of the true church of God, and of the spotless character of its true ministry—above all, of its sinless Head.

Blue-red

Foremost among the true colors of the Tabernacle was what in common parlance may be called "blue," but was in reality a mixture of *indigo-blue* with *deep-red*. So also was the next color (they are always named in the same order),[7] the difference being that in the former the blue predominated, in the latter the red. These two are the only instances of a compound color occurring in the whole description (except the implied brown and gray noticed above), and

---

one of them especially (*antilope barbatus*) is said to bear the closely similar name of *tachassè* in the native dialect of the interior of Asia. The use of *tachash*-skin for shoes (Ezek. 16:10) is not in reference to coarse sandals, but to a soft material for ladies' wear. In the absence of a definite identification, we cannot securely seek for the symbolical import further than to presume that the fur was fine and beautiful. The rougher and stronger external skin was colored for artistic effect, and afforded a rich contrast to the dark roof and the yellow planks. Beyond this it is not worthwhile to pursue the symbolism.

7. Atwater observes (*The Sacred Tabernacle,* p. 284, note): "The colors of the [wall] curtain called *the tabernacle* are always mentioned in the order which follows, namely, fine-twined linen, blue, purple, and crimson; but in all other cases, including the three veils and the sacerdotal garments, the colors are enumerated as blue, purple, crimson, and fine-twined linen. No one has suggested a reason for the difference of arrangement." One of these statements is not strictly correct, for in Exodus 39:29, the colors of the high priest's girdle are enumerated in the same order as those of the wall curtains, namely, "fine-twined linen, and blue, and purple, and scarlet." This shows that no special significance attaches to the position of the white, except in its relation to the gold, and so long as the other three colors are in their proper order, as they invariably are. Indeed it proves that the white was not a stripe at all, for in the description of the girdle of the ephod

they serve to show that no scientific analysis of rays is regarded. Green, it will be noticed, is altogether excluded, notwithstanding its abundance in nature, and its pleasant effect upon the eye, especially in a verdureless desert. Perhaps because it is suggestive of the earth, and hence too worldly, and also because it is almost exclusively vegetable. Blue, however, especially of the warm violet shade, is eminently characteristic of heaven (the cerulean sky, with a reddish tinge prevalent in the Orient), and hence interpreters, as by common consent, have not failed to recognize the symbolism here. "Blue" was used alone, to indicate the unalloyed serenity of the celestial world, the topmost goal of human aspiration; or in alternate stripes (never co-mingled, except with the white light that underlies and transfigures it) of more gorgeous hues, to intimate the successive stages of terrestrial life and station, through which mortals must pass in order to attain it.

Purple

The Tyrian *purple* of antiquity was universally accepted as the

---

(which we can hardly suppose to have been different in this respect from the principal girdle) the white occupies again the last place (28:8; 39:5). This is also corroborated by the fact that a similar variation occurs as to the relative order of the gold embroidery in the two accounts of the curtain for the court entrance (27:16; 38:18). The reason why the linen is named first in these two instances only (the curtains twice, 26:1; 36:8; and the principal girdle once, 39:29) seems to be the great length of these pieces of cloth (the longitudinal threads being of that material) as compared with the others. In the account of the same colors used in Solomon's Temple (2 Chron. 2:7, 14), the order is not at all observed, except as to the inner veil (3:14; because in that piece of cloth alone was it then employed, as there were no side curtains. We may further remark that the regular order, by which the gold (or its equivalent, the embroidery) is mentioned first, and the linen last (whenever these occur at all), is never varied except when, as in the cases of the linen noticed, and that of the gold already cited, the ground and figured colors are enumerated in the aspect of *materials* in bulk or in process of manufacture, rather than as made up articles (so the gold last, in the account of the contributions, 25:4; 28:5; 35:6, 23; of the men's work, 35:35; 38:23; of the ephod, 39:2, 3; of the breastplate, 28:15; 39:8). The addition of "linen" to the list of pomegranates in 39:24 (where "twined" refers to the colored threads), is a mistake of the A.V. (comp. 28:33). The order of the words in question, therefore, while everywhere true to the symbolism, is nowhere mystical or cabalistic.

emblem of royalty, which in some countries had the legal monopoly of it, as among the Mohammedans green is the exclusive badge of a lineal descendant of the prophet. It is, therefore, so appropriate to the mansion and servitors of the supreme King that we need not dwell upon it. It stands between the blue-red and the deep-red, as its shade naturally requires, and suggests that royalty, as yet unknown to the Hebrew polity, should eventually come as a mediator between God (in the azure heavens) and man (of the copper-colored flesh);[8]—a human viceregent of divine authority, and a Victim with a two-fold nature and dignity.

Crimson

The remaining shade of red, therefore, *crimson* (not "scarlet," which is too bright and flame-color to suit the shade and symbolism), or cochineal-red,[9] can only point to blood, shading off from its arterial hue (that here especially denoted as freshly shed), through the purplish color of raw flesh, into the bluish cast of the veins, but everywhere in the Scriptures designating the life-principle of man and beast (Gen. 9:4-6), and the essential element of atonement (Heb. 9:22). Here is a wide field for scientific and religious investigation, to which we forbear to do more than introduce the reader, leaving him to explore it with the copious aids easily available to him. Dr. H. Clay Trumbull, former editor of the *Sunday School Times,* has collected a mass of information on the widespread and deep relations of blood in the religious beliefs and customs of ancient and modern nations, in his interesting and valuable work, entitled, *The Blood Covenant,* which is in complete harmony with the pertinence of the symbol in this connection.

Yellow

The gold so lavishly bestowed upon the Tabernacle, both solid

---

8. It is noteworthy that *adám* ("man") and *adamáh* ("ground") both mean *red,* i.e., deep flesh-color, which is also that of unburnished and yet untarnished copper.

9. The Hebrew explicitly identifies it with a worm.

and laminated as well as in threads, and perhaps likewise, as we have surmised, in the silken stitches of the embroidery, yields the remaining color, *yellow,* which is obviously symbolical of the sun, as the great source of light (white) and heat (bright red as in flame). It may be observed that fire, which is a sort of orange, or mixture of red and yellow, is not represented here, perhaps on account of the dangerous tendency to its worship in the East. Through the metal, however, as the standard of coinage, it becomes the emblem of valuation.

We have seen that the three wool-colors, violet, purple and crimson, are always in the same order, and we have presumed that they were invariably thus placed on the door screens and elsewhere, reading, no doubt, after the Hebrew style, from right to left. Is it too great a stretch of fancy to suppose that this too is significant? Perhaps it symbolizes, first, the all-embracing and all-covering sky, for the horizon bounds every view laterally, and the zenith every one vertically. Second, that royalty is the next form or supremacy, the celestial Sovereign being above all. Third, that blood is the basis of unity in race and sympathy; and hence the universal Lord becomes incarnate for man. The background and overlay of gold intimates the price of human redemption, both as originally provided, and as eventually paid; and the ground color, white, points to the spiritual purity which is the origin and aim of the whole scheme of the *Atonement.* We may then translate the entire hieroglyph thus: HEAVEN'S ROYAL BLOOD PURCHASES PURITY. In the Hebrew idiomatic arrangement of words the significance would be equally apt and emphatic, and the form as precisely tallying in epigrammatic conciseness, for the five substances (or rather colors) are invariably named (when mentioned together in this connection) in the same order ("gold, and-violet-[wool], and-purple-[wool], and-crimson-[wool], and-bleached-[linen]"), so as to compose symbolically the ideogram, which we will endeavor to represent in English equivalents thus, *Yiqnú hash-shamáyim mim-malke-hém be-dam-ó eth-tohorath-énu,* literally, *Will-buy the-heavens from-their-King by-his-blood our-cleansing,* i.e., *Heaven will procure of its King our purification with His own blood.* The sacrifice of the God-man upon the cross is the only ransom of the human race from sin and its divinely pronounced penalty.

Expressed Hebraistically as a *rebus,* the elements will stand as in the following table. It may be observed that the three great realms of nature are all represented. 1. The mineral (as basic) by the first substance. 2. The animal (as most important) by the next and principal three (the sea, as being most populous, by two; and the air by one). and 3. The vegetable by the last: the hues begin with a faint one, and end with the mildest; while the intermediate ones are brilliant, in the order of the intensity of this strongest tint (red); the earth, with its (mixed but predominant) color green, as elsewhere noted, is studiously ignored in expression; but with its living tribes is everywhere supposed in fact. The first, the middle and the last thought are abstract, the other two concrete (the second divine, the fourth human); each thus linked together: the initial purpose is redemption, the central one supremacy (of the God-man), the final one holiness. This central legend, emblazoned on every avenue to the divine Majesty, and also on the person of the pontifical mediator, silently proclaimed with celestial rays (Ps. 19:1-4), the grand secret of the one true faith, devised in the eternal counsels of the Almighty (Col. 1:26, 27). It is the gospel of the Tabernacle, and a fit culmination of the symbolism of the entire edifice and its paraphernalia. It is the germinal idea at the core of this architectonic embodiment of the Levitical worship, the perpetual countersign of all real members of the universal Church, and the keynote in the everlasting song of the redeemed (Rev. 5:9, 10). It is the one essential doctrine both of Judaism and of Christianity, the cardinal fact foreshadowed in the former and realized in the latter. Like the prismatic bow of the first covenant with the second progenitor of our race (Gen. 9:13), and like the mystic ladder of Israel's dream (Gen. 28:12), it bridges the void between heaven and earth. It may be reserved for modern science to descry in its variegated bands the spectrum that shall disclose something of the inner nature of that far-off world, where, in His glorified humanity, the divine Son is preparing the home of His saints.

Order	1	2	3	4	5
Hebrew name	*Zaháb*	*Tekéleth*	*Argamán*	*Shaní*	*Shesh*
Object	Gold	Cerulean Mussel	Tyrian Conch	Oak Fly	Linen
Color	Yellow	Violet	Purple	Crimson	White
Idea	Price	Heaven	Royalty	Blood	Purity

As the width of the successive colored stripes is not given (they were doubtless co-equal in each piece of stuff), we have taken the liberty of varying them in this respect so as to suit the panels or spaces which they were intended to fill. It is a very remarkable coincidence that the violet falls exactly in the plain panel for the cherubim on the interior wall curtains. It is interesting to find, moreover, that in the arrangement of the folds the violet loops are always attached to the corners of the violet panels, as congruity requires. Moreover, every hanging begins and ends with violet— heaven being the source and aim of the Atonement. The white linen foundation speaks of the purity and strength that underlie the whole plan of redemption.

Even the color of the superimposed embroidery is in harmony with the above symbolism, for as yellow is the emblem of the sun, this orb, the fourth element in the cosmical system, fitly wanders over the face of the others, especially of the blue sky, not only calling into being the (vegetable) forms of beauty (vines, etc.) but also personifying the (animal) powers of nature (the cherubim).

It is noteworthy that as the temples and persons of the Egyptian and Assyrian monuments are figured all over with significant inscriptions, so the drapery of the Tabernacle and its high priest is thoroughly pictured with this central lesson of the redemptive plan.

EXTERNAL ASPECTS OF TABERNACLE ARTICLES

The remaining element of objects in and about the Tabernacle, that strikes the sense of sight as well as that of touch, is figure, and this we will consider as it relates both to mathematical form and to general shape,—the one a conventional or utilitarian sort of distinction, and the other a popular and aesthetical one, yet both blended in actual occurrence.

Geometrical Forms

Angular figures are mostly artificial, and therefore predominate in the mechanism of the Tabernacle, especially the rectangle, and this chiefly as a square, for the triangle appears but occasionally, as the bisection or diagonal of the quadrilateral. This figure is evidently the symbol of regularity, and leads us back to the idea of perfect proportion, with which we set out in this part of our discussion. The cube or third multiple of the same dimension, however, is rarely if at all found, except in the "tabernacle" part of the Most Holy Place, perhaps because it is monotonous. The oblique parallelogram is altogether avoided, as being unshapely.

More difficult of construction (without the contrivance of the lathe), and yet more abundant in nature, is the *round figure,* whether plane or spherical. This is fairly frequent in the Tabernacle apparatus, although never explicitly stated. It is the type of symmetry, every point of the periphery being equidistant from the center. To make it symbolical of the planetary bodies would be to anticipate the Copernican system.

Of the three simplest figures, namely, the circle, the triangle, and the quadrangle, representing respectively the unit as an emblem of eternity, the triad is as an emblem of strength, and the parallelogram as an emblem of convenience. The first and the last appear in the symbolism of the Tabernacle as representatives of perfect form from opposite points of view suitable to their nature: namely, the one subjectively from within, as a type of self-poised independent completeness, in the pillars, the laver, and certain details of the apparatus; the other objectively from without, in the superficial arrangement of the apartments, and the shape of certain pieces of manufacture. Their respective solid forms, the sphere and the cube, are of rare occurrence. The former, which is the proper symbol of Deity, and therefore not to be graphically represented (according to the second commandment), scarcely appears at all (for even the pomegranates and the bells are imperfect models). The latter appears only in the inmost shrine, the very abode of Deity, and thus the appropriate type, not only of heaven itself (into which Christ has finally entered, and whither His redeemed shall follow Him), but also of the as yet invisible Church (whither under Christianity all the saints are even now admitted as priests each for himself).

The two altars are squares, but not cubes, as if denoting a minor degree of perfection. The offerings, whether external and physical (like animal victims) or internal and spiritual (like clouds or incense) are limited (at least on earth) by the natural infirmities of the saints. The individual planks of the walls, which may symbolize the "living stones" of the true Temple, are accordingly rectangular merely, as being finite components of the divine abode. The outer apartments (holy place, sanctuary as a whole, and entire court) are for the same reason emblematic of this earthly state of existence and worship, which will be dispensed with in the celestial Temple by the occupants of "houses not made with hands, eternal in the heavens." Yet even the earthly fane was not absolutely perfect either for divine residence or worship, for it was surmounted by the prismatic peak, which pointed skyward to the superincumbent cloud as the place of the continual immanence of deity, rather than to the occasional Shekinah below. The outer room, of course, denoted a less degree of the divine presence, as to the unconsecrated or nominal worshiper, and the outer court even less, as to the lay or Gentile world. The former is still under the shade of the sacred vocation, and the latter only under the broad canopy of heaven's general covenant. The triangle is of infrequent occurrence, and its solid, the pyramid, seems to have been avoided as an Egyptian type of stability, both hybrid (for the base is not triangular) and inapposite (for the Tabernacle was neither stationary nor perpetual.

The most unique of the forms introduced among the accessories of the Tabernacle is that of the *cherubim,* and, although purely symbolical, they have accordingly been the greatest puzzle to interpreters, who have often taken the most unwarrantable liberties in guessing their significance. We venture to expound them as cosmical emblems of the divine attributes, or as modern science (somewhat atheistically, we fear) styles them, "the laws of nature." They are the creative and providential functions of God, exercised in behalf of His human subjects through the agency—not of angels (who are actual persons, i.e., free moral beings), as the Scriptures represent to be done in the supernatural relations of the world, but of special imaginary beings, invented for this sole purpose, in the national and ecclesiastical spheres. Accordingly, they are depicted as having a material form, and an animated existence; as invested with a human body, yet ruddy as polished copper, not feathered, except probably on the wings; nor hairy, except, of course, on the head, and possibly about the feet; as standing on the cloven feet and upright (pliable) legs of a ceremonially "clean" creature, to which free locomotion is secured if needed, or a firm position when at rest. They possess arms for convenient and efficient service, and likewise wings for independent transportation, the latter double for the purpose of a garment. (The consentaneous "wheels" of Ezekiel, to denote a support to the divine throne, with their felloes of eyes [in Rev. 4:6, 8, the eyes are many, and on the person], denoting vigilance in every direction, are a later device of the theophantic machinery.) The four faces (the countenance being the distinctive feature by which to recognize individuals) are the main index of their typical significance. The human denotes intelligence, the leonine strength, the bovine perseverance, and the aquiline rapidity.

Even the relative position of the four faces of the cherubim appears to be significant: the human, as is befitting the lord of creation, occupying the front; the leonine, as king of the lower orders, ranking next on the right; the bovine, as chief of the domestic animals, supporting on the left; and the aquiline, as prince of the air, bringing up the rear. As symbolical of the laws of nature, the fourfold aspect of the cherubim is neither arbitrary nor accidental, but points to every quarter of the earth (comp. Job 23:8, 9; Zech. 6:1-8), whither they are the vehicles of sovereign Providence, acting with the far-reaching aim of sagacity, the right hand of efficiency, the left of persistency, and the pinions of celerity; and with these essential attributes all their members correspond. Ever since the fall of man they forefend his acess to the elixir of life by the sword of mortality brandished outward in the three directions of disease, accident and old age. They garrison the Church impregnably against all assaults (comp. Matt. 16:18), standing on guard at the portal of the King of kings, and presiding over the depositary of His statutes; they are specially subsidized in every ecclesiastical crisis (as in the book of Ezekiel), although they only appear to the inspired eye (comp. 2 Kings 6:17), and they will not cease their ministry till the close of time (Rev. 4:6-9, etc.).

This gives us a complete picture of an omniscient, omnipotent, uniform and ubiquitous maintenance and superintendence of the external fortunes and affairs of the body of true worshipers, i.e., the Church in all time.

It need occasion neither alarm nor surprise, if the early preconceptions of these singular forms have to be brushed aside by the rigid facts of prosaic analysis and cool exegesis, but the love of truth compels us to dismiss all such vague and chimerical ideas. We must ever bear in mind that the forms were intended not to amuse but to symbolize, to delight the spiritual apprehension rather than to fascinate the eye. All sensuous imagery would have savored of idolatry; and this the sacredness of the shrine most intensely abhorred. Furthermore, modern notions have largely confounded cherubim with *angels,* although in the Scriptures the two are widely different in character, function, and representation. The latter are properly embodiments of personal and moral agents, real beings; the former are merely exponents of ideal and natural qualities, configurations not only nonexistent but impossible in fact. The cherubim are undraped save by wings, in order to denote their original simplicity of sentiment and their nonconformity to artificial fashions.

Angels, on the contrary, in the Scriptures always have appeared in the ordinary costume of men, even if with a halo. In the passage usually cited in support of the winged form of angels (Dan. 9:21), Gabriel is explicitly called a "man," nor is there the slightest intimation of his otherwise than perfect human form. The phrase "being caused to fly swiftly," is a curious instance of alliteration, *mûâph bîâph,* which may be rendered literally, "made to fly with weariness," i.e., having suddenly arrived with the fatigue of a long journey. The former word is frequently used in the metaphorical sense of rapid motion, irrespective of wings, and the latter word has no connection with flying. Both words are evidently taken somewhat out of their ordinary meaning, for the sake of agreement in sound. Indeed the best Hebraists derive them both from the same word—and that the latter one, which is grammatically the more probable, both from its form and the idiom—and render the clause "utterly weary." Thus all trace of winged angels disappears from the Scriptures; for the locomotion in Revelation 8:13 and 14:6, was a special adaptation, as in 12:14. Other instances adduced (Judg. 13:20; Ps. 104:4; Isa. 6:2; Matt. 28:3) are not to the point.

As to the seemingly uncouth combination of animal and human elements in the cherubic figures, our prejudices must give way before the plain descriptions of the Bible, and the delineations of contemporary religions. The monuments of Egypt and Assyria frequently represent similar custodians of palaces, temples and sacred rites as having feathered wings and a bird's beak, and in other emblematic carvings in like cases a human face surmounts the body of a bull or a lion. Sometimes a more ignoble beast, or even a fish or a serpent is pressed into service. Pagan mythology is full of such hybrid forms. The sphinx is one of the most notable riddles of antiquity. Nobody imagines that such creatures actually existed. The scriptural cherubim are a great improvement upon even the classical models, and their very oddity renders their significance the more striking.

The substantially *human* form likewise of those occult figures, the Urim and Thummim, can scarcely be doubted after an examination of the passages where they are referred to, and especially upon a comparison with the teraphim of the Hebrews and the images of the Egyptian shrines. The reader, however, will observe that the genuine ones are never mentioned in the Mosaic account as objects of worship, but only as a sort of talisman for divination. At this focal point of the sacerdotal apparatus, therefore, we again meet with almost striking premonition of the *atonement,* which links earth to heaven, and allies God with man; not now, as in the sacred colors, which are an aspect of the vicarious sacrifice for man before God, but in the theanthropic shape, which bodies forth the Deity before man, as the other great design of the assumption of flesh by the Son of God. Jesus is not only *the* light (*ûr*) of the world (John 1:5, 9; 8:12), but the sole perfect (*thûm*) human being, who reveals the divine nature and purposes (John 1:18), not alone by His person, which is the express image of the Father, but also in His life, which is the effulgence of His glory,—not simply by His precepts, which are infallible truth, but likewise by His example, which is the complete pattern for all saints. If we are correct in supposing that the object in the pectoral pocket of the high priest was in fact single, although in name, for the sake of superlative emphasis, both double and plural, then this sole and peerless God-man, who once disclosed His innate splendor to the privileged three on the mount of transfiguration, and occasionally gave glimpses of His beatified glory, as to the protomartyr and to the preeminent apostle, is the real and apt antitype of this divining symbol as well as of the Shekinah between the cherubim. The same will be finally gazed upon, as the attraction of the true temple, and the unsetting sun of the new heavens, by all the devout there forever recognized as "kings and priests unto God."

It was for worship that the Tabernacle itself was erected, in place of the casual, isolated and impromptu devotion of persons or families, with whatever rites or in whatever order each might see fit, whether borrowed from traditions or profane sources, or dictated by caprice or fashion. So essential is a meeting house that it has at length taken the name of a "church." So useful is a ritual that even non-liturgical communions have adopted some conventional order of service. If they succeed in retaining the divine supervision symbolized in the cherubic guards, they may promise themselves permanence and success in the earth. Nevertheless, it is only by preserving the spiritual baptism prefigured in the fire of the Cloud, the Altar and the Shekinah, that they can hope to fit the souls of their membership for the inward communion either here or hereafter.

The varied postures of the upper set of cherubic wings, to which we have previously called attention, remain to be expounded. On the wall drapery, where the figures are entirely stationary, we have conceived the wings as being folded nearly vertically[10] (as described in Ezek. 1:24, 25, "When they stood, they [not "and had"] let down their wings"). This seems to denote the quiescent attitude of the cherubim there as the fixed custodians of the holy apartments. On the Veil, however, where they are raised a cubit from the ground, in mid-air, so to speak, of course they would be represented as flying. Their wings are extended horizontally, in order to touch those of the adjoining cherub (as described again in Ezek. 1:9, 11 [render "parted from as to upward," instead of "stretched upward," i.e., separated at the top outwardly from the body], 23, 24), like active sentinels, barring the passageway. Not now armed, as in Genesis 3:24, but allowing the high priest to enter, yet not without his raising the Veil, and thus for the moment displacing them.

Finally, over the Ark, on the lid on which they stand,[11] and yet are raised as high from the ground as on the Veil, the cherubims are

---

10. Probably over the other pair, so that, as on the Egyptian monuments, they appear as if having but two.

11. The Ark was closed by a lid, not as a sign of secrecy (for the Law was proclaimed with the most portentous publicity), but in token of inviolate safety and perpetuity; and the cordon of cherubs was significant of the same guaranty. The Shekinah glow occasionally vouchsafed upon it, as a mark of the divine acceptance of the "blood of sprinkling, that speaketh better things than that of Abel" (Heb. 12:24, the one calling for vengeance against the fratricide, the other for pardon; see Luke 23:34), when offered by the devout high priest as a representative of his people, was a message of "mercy glorying over justice" (as we may properly render James 2:13; comp. Ps. 85:10) symbolized by the Decalogue lying below it. This justification, which takes place in the arcana of heaven, is testified to the worshiper without by the spirit of adoption (Rom. 8:15, 16; Gal. 4:6), which the ascended Advocate has sent into the hearts of believers (John 16:7) as a notice of His own triumphant reception within the Veil (Acts 2:33; Heb. 10:12).

in the act of alighting. Therefore, they lift their wings somewhat higher, face one another, and bend their arms embracingly towards the Mercy Seat (Exod. 25:20), as if it were their nest. This central object of the whole economy of the Tabernacle affords a most signal example of the casual and inaccurate style current in the interpretation of the symbolism of the entire subject from the earliest time to the present day. The lid of the Ark has been made an emblem of divine reconciliation without the slightest foundation for the conceit. The prominence and universality of this error deserve a detailed refutation.

Philologically considered the Hebrew word *kappóreth* is a feminine participial noun from *kaphár,* which means to "cover," and, therefore, signifies merely a *covering* or "lid" to the box. It is used of this article only, because none of the other pieces of furniture or utensils had a movable cover. The Septuagint version translated it by the Greek term *hilastérion,* which means "propitiatory." The Latin Vulgate imitated the rendering by *propitiatorium,* and the later versions have heedlessly adopted the same idea, as in the Authorized English "mercy seat," which the Revised Version has retained. Hence a world of mistaken sentiment and false poetry has been freely constructed throughout Christendom by allusions to this supposed symbol, based upon a sheer blunder of translation. It is true, the verb, especially in the *Piel* or intensive conjugation, from which this word is immediately derived, often has the figurative sense of *covering up* or pardoning sin. This very rarely occurs, however, without express mention of guilt and a preposition to connect the object with the verb, and thus point out the figurative

---

The material on which the Decalogue was inscribed was an emblem of its formal rigidity (see 2 Cor. 3:3, 7), the number of its tables indicated the trustworthiness of its testimony (see Deut. 17:6), their engraving on both sides was expressive of its full significance (comp. Rev. 5:1), and its square form denoted its perfection (comp. Rev. 21:16). The divine autograph was a seal of its direct authority, which even the Son has never abrogated (see Matt. 5:17, 18).

The disappearance of the autograph tables of the Decalogue after the destruction of the Temple by the Babylonians was the signal for a more earnest study of the Law by the Jews, which ensured its transferral to their minds so as never again to be forgotten, in letter at least (Jer. 31:33).

relation. The Most Holy Place is once (1 Chron. 28:11) styled "the house of the *kappóreth,*" but this was never a distinctive or prominent title of the building or the apartment. In David's time, However, it may naturally have been used for the home about to be prepared for the long houseless Ark itself, of which the *kappóreth* was so conspicuous a part. There is no sufficient linguistic reason for departing from the obvious literal meaning of the word here, as denoting a cover to the chest.

Exegetically regarded, nothing could be more inappropriate than the notion of any piacular or atoning quality or reference in the lid of the Ark or anything connected with it. True, it was the seat of the divine Shekinah, when present; but this was occasional only, accessible to the high priest solely, but once a year at that, and deterrent when it did occur (see 1 Kings 8:11). The cherubim that stood upon it were in like manner forbidding rather than inviting; for, as at the gate of Paradise, they were designed to warn off all intruders; and with a like intent the Ark itself was closed from all inspection by the cover in question. Privacy and severity were the regnant principles in the entire arrangement of this article most especially. There is not the slightest hint that clemency or pardon was signified, but, on the contrary, the most rigid seclusion and inexorable justice. The high priest himself was not allowed to approach it in his robes of office, but as a culprit doomed to degradation and death. Inaccessibility and sternness were its chief or only lessons. Such passages as Exodus 25:22, which speak of communication from that spot, have reference to Moses exclusively.

Authoritatively expounded, we are not at liberty to appeal to the apostle's allusion in the Epistle to the Hebrews (9:5, where the popular term *hilastérion* is employed, but without any special stress or interpretation). The context shows that the main purpose of the reference is to bring out a contrast in this respect between the Jewish "mercy seat" and the Christian, rather than to make the former symbolical of the latter. Thus, whether we consider the rent veil as the separation between this world and the other as regards the glorified Redeemer in heaven, or His justified believers on earth, it is emphatically true that Christians only are privileged to enter the sacred presence with assurance of welcome (Heb. 10:19-22). The true and only *propitiatorium* is the person of Jesus Christ (Rom. 3:25; comp. Heb. 2:17; 1 John 2:2; 4:10). This cannot with any propriety be symbolized by the Ark, for although the sprinkling with blood occurred in connection with both, yet in the case of Jesus it was His own blood poured forth upon His own body, while the Ark had no blood of its own, and the victim's did not actually come in contact with it all (as we have shown above). The arguments adduced in favor of the popular view by a writer are insufficient to countervail these objections. The only sense in which the idea of a *propitiatory* could be entertained, consistently with sound Christian typology, would be the local one of a favored spot where Jehovah deigned to show Himself in token of special approbation of the worship rendered Him. For this thought the term "throne" would have been more appropriate, a meaning which cannot be extracted from *kappóreth,* although it is implied in the word *yoshéb,* sometimes used by the sacred writers in poetical passages alluding to the sanctuary (lit. "the[One] sitting between the cherubim," etc.). Among eminent Jewish and Christian scholars, some are still in favor of the rendering "mercy seat" (so Kalisch, Lange, Keil, Michaelis, Tholuck, and a few others); but the great majority of the best linguists and interpreters favor the simpler version "lid" (so De Wette, Gesenius, Fürst, Schott, Zunz, Knobel, Herxheimer, Leeser, Benisch, Sharpe, Delitzsch, Kuinöl, Winer, and many others); some are undecided (Rosenmüller, Ewald, Hengstenberg, etc.).

The cherubims' interest gradually deepens and intensifies in the sacred deposit entrusted to their care amid the darkness, the silence and the loneliness of the Holy of Holies, and at length they hover over it with the affection of foster parents. Throned within this triple line of mystical guards, the blazing symbol of the King of kings occasionally deigned to manifest itself to the favored but representative worshiper, in all that mortal eyes could bear of the divine glory (Exod. 33:18-23; 34:5-8), while overhead perpetually hung the milder token of Jehovah's presence before the public gaze, in the nimbus[12] alternately white and glowing.

Its Preservation

In the sacred Ark, although designated by a different term from that of Noah,[13] we may still recognize the common idea of preservation: in the present case as a depository of the divinely-given tables of the moral law;[14] in the other as a temporary receptacle for such of the animal tribes of the vicinity as could not otherwise be readily reproduced. The significant manner in which an apostle alludes to the flood (2 Peter 2:5; 3:6) seems to have led the framers of the baptismal service in the English Prayer Book to regard Noah's ark as typical (for it is there associated with the passage of the Red Sea, as if likewise "prefiguring Holy Baptism"). Be that as it may, Noah's ark, as being the very first inhabited structure known to have been planned by the Almighty Architect, it might be presumed, however different its design, to offer some points of analogy to the Tabernacle at least, and possibly to the Ark under consideration. It is, therefore, worth our while to make a brief comparison.

COMPARISON OF THE THREE ARKS

The dimensions of the Noachian edifice (for such it was before being launched by the Deluge) are given likewise in cubits; namely, 300 long, 50 wide and 30 high (about the proportions of a large merchant ship of the present day), which (with the exception of the length, which in a sea vessel must always be relatively greater than

---

12. Hebrew *anán,* the dense thunder-cloud, loaded with the refreshing shower, yet charged with the electric flashes.

13. Hebrew *tebáh,* a foreign word, probably signifying a "chest," and used only of this vessel and of the basket in which Moses was enclosed (Exod. 2:3, 5), both intended to float on the water. It is not a little singular that on the Egyptian monuments the shrine and a boat are so often associated together.

14. That this was the simple purpose of the Ark is evident from Deuteronomy 10:1, 2; indeed from v. 3 it seems that the Ark was prepared in advance. This was the peerless jewel of the entire casket and treasure-house.

that of a house—for the latter would not stand securely if so narrow) are not greatly out of ratio with those of the Tabernacle walls (30 × 10 × 10), nor with those of the Tabernacle Ark ($2\frac{1}{2}$ × $1\frac{1}{2}$ × $1\frac{1}{2}$). Noah's ark had three stories, the Tabernacle one and one half, and its Ark properly but one; showing a gradual reduction in this regard. As we are not informed what partitions, if any, were made in the successive floors of Noah's ark, we can not compare it in this regard with the Tabernacle or its Ark. We may presume, however, that there was a corresponding decrease in their number. Internal decorations, of course, are out of the question in the case of both the other arks. The contents, however, were in a certain sense germinal in all three; the first contained the vital seeds of a new population for the globe, the second the hero-nucleus of a fresh nation, and the third the essential principles of all morality.

It is in the architectural style of the three structures that we would naturally expect to find the greatest degree of conformity, as emanating from the same Mind. Thus we are not disappointed. All three were essentially a rectangular box (neglecting the tent-roof of the Tabernacle, which was properly no part of the wooden *mishkán* or "dwelling"). Plain, indeed, was this form for a ship, and not very artistic perhaps for a house. Yet it was admirably adapted, in fact, to all of these uses, the first to be floated, the second to be "pitched," and the third to be simply set down. The roof, which we have just laid out of the account, presents, nevertheless, some very curious points of resemblance. Although flat, of course, in the case of the Mercy Seat, it must have been more or less sloping in the Noachian ark, as in the Tabernacle, to carry off the rain. At the eaves, especially, we find recurring an arrangement remarkably similar, and yet characteristically different, for the purpose of shedding the drip. The bottom cubit of the roof material all around, which in the Tabernacle was turned down over the top of the walls, was here carried out as a cornice or projection, and left an opening of that width in the top of the side walls, for light and ventilation (Gen. 6:16). "A window [Heb. *tsóhar,* a "light," used only of this object, and in the dual of *noon;* a different word is employed in 8:6] shalt thou make to the ark, and in [rather "to," lit. "toward"] a cubit shalt thou finish it [the ark, not the window, as the gender shows] above [rather "from the top downward," lit. "from as to upward," the identical expression applied to the same space in the Tabernacle (Exod. 26:14)]." This space, where the boarding-up of the sides was omitted, was protected from the rain by the over-jutting eaves. In this opening was set the lattice,[15] which Noah first opened to let the raven and the dove out and in (Gen. 8:6), and through which, as it was situated at the ceiling of the top story,[16] he could see the towering tops of the surrounding mountains (v. 5). It was only after the return of the dove with a fresh olive leaf in her mouth, which assured him that the ground was sufficiently dry to warrant him in doing so (v. 11), without danger of swamping his vessel in some valley, that he ventured to take off part of the side boarding itself,[17] and then for the first time actually *saw* that the ground was thoroughly dry (v. 13). This explanation so fairly clears up this difficult passage, and at the same time so corroborates our view of the Tabernacle, that we trust the reader will pardon what otherwise might seem to be unnecessary digression. (See Fig. 37.)

The ark of bulrushes (i.e., papyrus reeds), in which the infant Moses was placed by his mother (designated as we have seen above by the same word as the ark of Noah), is significant likewise of preservation, and has many other features of similarity. It was a wicker box of about the same proportions as the average noticed above, being shaped like a sarcophagus or mummy-case, coated too with bitumen inside and out (corresponding to the plating on

---

15. Hebrew *chalón* (lit. a *perforation*, A.V. "window"), constantly used of latticed openings in the side of Oriental buildings.

16. We conceive that the middle floor of the ark, being dark and chilly, was occupied with provisions for the animals, while the hold would make an excellent cistern for fresh water (filled by the 40 days' rain) necessary not only for use during the whole year's confinement, but also for ballast.

17. Hebrew *mikséh,* "covering," the very word exclusively applied elsewhere to the outside blanket of fur on the Tabernacle walls. Perhaps the exact part here referred to was the door in the side of the ark (of course, in the bottom story), which was fastened on the outside (6:16; 7:16), as was necessary in order to resist the pressure of water, which during the Flood would be very great.

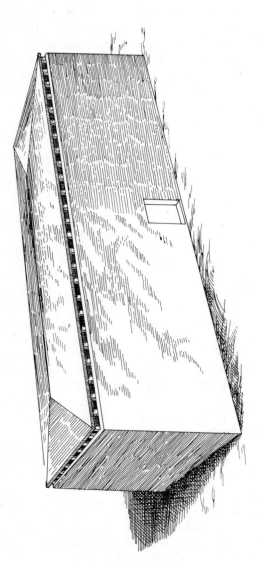

Fig. 37.—Restoration of Noah's Ark

the boards of the Tabernacle and the Ark of the Covenant), draped with the babe's clothing, and requiring for his breathing an opening around the top of the floating cradle of the future law giver similar to that of the Noachian ark, effected doubtless by the omission of some of the longitudinal courses of wattles. (See Fig. 38.)

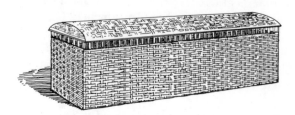

Fig. 38.—Probable form of the Ark of Bulrushes

THE DECALOGUE

In the tables of the Decalogue deposited within the sacred Ark we, at once, recognize the symbols of moral law, not now for the first time promulgated—for the sins against God and the crimes against man there prohibited have always been outlawed by the universal conscience. It was needful that these fundamental principles of ethics should be formally reestablished and authoritatively published to the newly-formed commonwealth of Israel. We perceive therefore that, while the ten commandments are specifically Jewish enactments, they are also cosmopolitan and perpetual statutes—"common law" as we now say. Nevertheless, in the theological sense no more a ground of salvation for fallen mn—who has already broken, and unaided can never keep them—than the ceremonial code of the Pentateuch is. They emphasize indeed certain principles of legislation, notably monotheism and the Sabbath, because these had been—and alas still are—sadly neglected. In the main they simply reiterate the cardinal rules of civilized society. They are all negative in substance—as was the first command in Eden, and as criminal behests usually are; and yet they attach no specific penalty, implying the extreme one of ecclesiastical excision and physical death. They are personal in application ("thou shalt"), and unmistakable in import. Finally, as our Lord expounded them (Matt. 5:21, 22, 28), and as the enlightened Jew easily discovered (Rom. 7:7-13), the meaning goes far deeper than the letter, and reaches to the spirit and intention of the soul (Heb. 4:12).

The typical character of the stone tablets is finely brought out even by Old Testament writers (Prov. 3:3; 7:3; Jer. 17:1; 31:33), but still more clearly by those of the New Testament (2 Cor. 3:3, 7; Heb. 8:10; 10:16), as contrasting with the tender receptivity of the heart. The breaking of those prepared by Jehovah Himself, as ominous of a covenant never fully renewed, is intimated in Moses' own premonitions of the frequent and final apostasy of his people (Deut. 9:7-24; 31:16-27).

The remaining features of the structure of the Tabernacle and its paraphernalia, such as the variety in the colors and arrangement of the drapery, the swellings in the stem and arms of the Candelabrum, the jewels and additions to the pontifical robes, etc., although in a degree useful, were chiefly ornamental. In that light they symbolize the element of beauty as one of the important constituents in this lesson-picture of Jehovah to His infant people. The aesthetic is never neglected by the divine Architect, nor was it sacrificed to utility in the somewhat severe style[18] of the Tabernacle, any more than it is in nature, where birds and flowers and graceful forms mingle in delightful harmony with the athletic forces and the rugged aspects of earnest existence. True science and chaste art are the legitimate twin offspring of genuine piety.

---

18. It is proper to observe that while the Tabernacle, both as a whole and in its details, can hardly be called elegant, as compared with the Temple and other gorgeous specimens of architecture, yet it was far from rude or out of taste. Indeed, not only eminent skill, but also great magnificence was displayed in its design and decorations, and the materials were often of the most costly character. The rich stuffs, precious metals and valuable gems lavished upon it were part of the "spoil" demanded by the Israelites as a just return from the Egyptians for long years of hard servitude (Exod. 12:35, 36). The means of keeping up the sacred services, such as flour, oil, etc., argue some communication with their settled neighbors during the long sojourn in the desert. Egypt is to this day the source of merchandise for the Arabs there. The mines of the Sinaitic peninsula were a noted penal station of the ancient Egyptians, and regular trains of supplies were kept up

SYMBOLISM OF TABERNACLE MATERIALS

Having thus nearly exhausted the external aspects of the Tabernacle equipments, we may properly inquire whether the various materials used in its constitution and operation may not likewise have some symbolical meaning. They are, as we have seen, drawn from all three kingdoms of nature, the mineral, the vegetable and the animal. We will take them up as nearly as may be in the order of their occurrence.

Wood

The largest in quantity of these materials, and that most used in dwellings, especially those intended for transportation like this, because furnishing the greatest strength for the least weight, is *wood*. In this instance it was taken from the acacia tree, not merely because this was the most—almost the only one—accessible in sufficient quantities, nor yet simply because it was firm and durable, but also because by reason of its terrific "touch-me-not" thorns that tree was a fit emblem of the unapproachable majesty of Jehovah, and of all that pertained to Him. The tree[19] is well described by Tristram:[20]

> There can be no question as to the identity of the *shittáh* with the acacia, the only timber tree of any size in the Arabian desert. The species of acacia found there is the *acacia seyal,* a gnarled and thorny tree, somewhat

for the military guards and convicts sent thither. These men were readily accessible to the Israelites, without danger of interference from the home government, now thoroughly reconciled to their emigration. Moses himself had the benefit of a forty years' experience as a refugee in this very region. The beaten caravan route from Damascus (Gen. 37:25) ran along the Philistine shore (Exod. 13:17). The crossline of pilgrimage to Mecca is comparatively modern, and does not touch Mt. Sinai, which, however, appears to have been an ancient shrine of religious resort (Exod. 3:1), as the inscribed rocks of its neighborhood seem to show. Its native population must always have been sparse and nomadic.

19. The Hebrew name for the *tree* is *shittáh* (fem. sing.), while for the *wood* it is *shittîm* (masc. plur., i.e., the sticks. (See Fig. 39.)

20. Tristram, H. B., *Natural History of the Bible,* p. 391-392.

Fig. 39.—The *Acacia Seyal* (tree, branch, flower, and pod).

like a solitary hawthorn in its habit and manner of growth, but much larger. It flourishes in the driest situations, and is scattered more or less numerously over the whole of the Siniatic peninsula. The timber is very hard and close grained, of a fine orange brown color, with a darker heart, and admirably adapted for fine cabinet work. Its leaves are small and pinnate, and in spring it is covered with its round tufts of yellow blossom, which grow in clusters round the branches, like little balls of fiber, and have gained for its poetical epithet of the "yellow-haired acacia." It belongs to the natural order *leguminosa,* and its seed is a pod like that of the laburnum.

But it is best known for its commercial value as yielding the gum arabic of trade and medicine, which is exported in great quantities from the Red Sea. The gum exudes from the tree spontaneously, as I have often observed in hot weather, but is also obtained more systematically by making incisions in the bark; and the Arabs not only collect it for sale, but for food in times of scarcity. They also say that it allays thirst. The bark, which is a powerful astringent, is used by the Bedouin for tanning yellow leather, and the camels are fed on its thorny foliage.

The burning bush of Moses (Exod. 3:2), called *seneh* in Hebrew, was no doubt an acacia, the Egyptian name of which is the equivalent, *sunt,* while the Arabic is *seyal.* The species is the *acacia nilotica,* found also in the desert, and rather smaller than the true seyal.

There are several other species of acacia found in Palestine, but all similar in habit and appearance; as the *acacia farnesiana* on the coast, the *a. serissa* in some of the wadies, and *a. tortilis* in some of the southern wadies. These must not be confounded with the tree commonly called acacia in England, which is an American plant of a different genus, with *white* papilionaceous blossoms—the *robinia pseudoacacia.*"

This was the symbolism likewise in the case of the burning bush that Moses saw in the same vicinity, which he was forbidden to

---

21. Hebrew *man hu, What* [is] *it?* A.V. incorrectly, "It is manna." Michael Liebentantz, in his little monograph on this subject (*De Manna Israelitarum,* 1667) nearly exhausted the sources of information (chiefly of a philological character) accessible in his day. The copy in our possession has mss. notes on the margin, apparently by the author himself. The true manna of the Desert is probably to be substantially identified, not with the medicinal substance current

approach (Exod. 3:5). May not the *manna*—that article of food so strange to the Hebrews that they had no name for it (Exod. 16:15),[21] but which we know was a type of Christ as the Bread of Life (John 6:31-35), may not this dew-like substance have been a preternatural exudation from this very tree? The strikingly similar and highly nutritive "gum arabic" of commerce is the natural one from at least one species of the same genus (with which they must have been well acquainted in Egypt).

The wood was employed in the Tabernacle chiefly for overlaying with metal, and was thus in a double sense a symbol of support, as it held up—whether naked or so covered—the textile portions of the tent-like structure. So the Israelites themselves—and all their fellow creatures, but more especially saints—are upheld naturally as well as spiritually—by that tree of life, invisible since Eden, which emblematized the alimentive and curative power of God (Rev. 21:2).

Metals

First mentioned among the metallic substances of the Tabernacle was *copper,* employed most copiously, not merely on account of its comparative cheapness, but rather for its deep color, and especially because it is capable (by some art now lost) of being hardened like steel,[22] and, therefore, the symbol of durability.

---

under that name among druggists, which is a saccharine cathartic exuding from certain species of the ash tree, but with the *gum arabic* of commerce, tons of which the writer saw piled in sacks on the banks of the Nile at Aswân, awaiting shipment down the river. There are several other Oriental trees which yield sweetish products often called manna, especially the *turfa* or tamarisk, distillations from which are collected in small quantities at Sinai, but form a syrup, not at all answering the biblical description, which moreover includes some miraculous features, especially the double quantity and the keeping quality on Friday, while none fell on the Sabbath.

22. Homer speaks (*Odyssey,* ix, 39; but some understand *iron*) of tempering copper for tools, and the Egyptians are thought (by Wilkinson, *Ancient Egyptians,* ii, 158) to have cut even the flinty Syenitic granite with it. They had extensive copper mines in the desert of Sinai, the refuse and pits of which are abundantly evident to this day at Surabet el-Khadim. They do not appear to have been acquainted with iron, and this metal accordingly does not find a place among the materials of the Tabernacle; nor would it have been suitable, from its liability to rust.

Next in order of dignity among metals, but used with much liberty in the Tabernacle, was *silver,* the obvious symbol of clearness, by its white lustre. Its employment for the trumpets is appropriate for the excellent tone thus produced, symbolical of the Gospel message (Ezek. 33:3; 1 Cor. 14:8; Rev. 8:6; 14:6).

The most costly metal, *gold,* was profusely employed about the Tabernacle, but wholly for inside work. As it is a universal standard, therefore, it is a symbol of value.

Cloth

Returning to the vegetable kingdom for the accessories of the Tabernacle structure and outfit, we find *linen,* or the product of the flax plant, most prominent for the hangings and clothing. It is a symbol of cleanliness, which, as the old proverb has it, is "next to godliness," and was a point of great concern in the sacred paraphernalia.

Next in importance for similar use was the *wool* of sheep, a ceremonially clean animal, evidently a symbol of warmth.

For canvas alone was the *goats' hair* (another "clean" animal) employed, which here seems to be a symbol of compactness, as the roof covering required that quality in an eminent degree.

The unshorn *rams' skins,* tinted for beauty, are a symbol of protection from weather.

The *fur blankets* were a symbol of softness. If they were of goats or antelopes, they likewise were from a "clean" animal. No further substance from the animal kingdom appears, except perhaps silk as an alternate for gold, and the red or crimson, likewise from a worm; finally, the two purples, from sea shells.

The *rope,* probably also of flaxen thread, used as stay cord, may be taken to represent strength, as linen twine is the least liable to break of any.

Stones

Finally, in this list of substances we set down, what are perhaps the most expensive of all for their size, the gems or *precious stones,* which, as they were to receive the engraving, may be regarded as a symbol of hardness.

Other Materials

Supplementary to the foregoing list, among elements employed in worship, we find *water*, as the symbol of regeneration; (perpetual) *fire*, as representing (quenchless) zeal; *oil*, as emblematic of richness; *wine*, of cheerfulness; *salt*, of wholesomeness; *flesh*, of substance; *fat*, of choice (as being the best part); *blood*, of life; *meal*, of vigor; and *spice*, of acceptability. Most of these are so frequent in the metaphors of the Bible that we need not dwell upon them in detail.

RELATIVE SANCTITY OF VARIOUS PARTS

A more noteworthy feature of the arrangement of the various parts of the Tabernacle, and one which we might have considered under the head of its relative proportions, but which we preferred to scrutinize a little more closely by itself, is the gradation of comparative or official sanctity manifested in the successive apartments and pieces of furniture.

In a general way it is obvious that the entire mansion and precincts are set forth as the residence of Jehovah in the style of an Oriental king, and that this was his special home among his chosen people. The successive door screens kept out all intruders, and the furniture was such as suited his royal state and convenience. In the courtyard were performed the culinary offices of the establishment, the food was cooked on the Brazen Altar, and the washing was done at the Laver. The Holy Place represented the reception room, where official business was transacted. Here the nightlong lamp denoted the ceaseless vigilance and activity of the Heavenly King. The Table of Shewbread was His board, furnished with the three principal articles of Oriental subsistence, bread, oil and wine. The Altar of Incense was the place appointed for the reception of homage and petitions from His subjects. The interior apartment was His secret chamber for His own private counsels and retirement.

After leaving the outside world of purely secular interests, we have first the large court accessible to all priests and Levites, but (except for individual privilege) to none others. The phrase, "door of the tent" [not "tabernacle"], so often used of the rendezvous of the people [i.e., of their representative heads] (Lev. 8:3, 4, etc.; but not when spoken of the priests), was merely outside the front screen of the court doorway, for it is the same word (*péthach,* lit. an *opening*) that is likewise applied to that of the building itself, but never to the inmost Veil. The enclosure, therefore, symbolizes a sacred ministry in more than the usual sense of God's people. Within this, again, we find the Laver, which is emblematic of true piety (such as can only flow from a renewed heart, Titus 3:5), and is placed there as an indispensable prerequisite to any acceptable divine service, especially of the priestly representatives of the people (Heb. 10:22). The Great Altar is a figure of the personal consecration which they are to make of their whole selves to holy duties.

In the next remove from secular life, the Holy Place, to which no Levite was ordinarily admitted, we see the exclusive tokens of a functional priesthood, which was necessary in the cumbrous and technical routine of sacrificial offerings, and was accordingly regarded as the only feasible medium of approach to the divine Majesty. Under the Gospel this whole system of human intervention is abolished, with the ritualistic system upon which it was founded, and every believer, whether old or young, male or female, becomes a king and a priest (for himself or herself only, however) before God (1 Peter 2:5, 9; Rev. 1:6, etc.) The Candelabrum represents the intelligence with which such service must be undertaken, the Table of Shewbread (lit. "of the [divine] presence") the conscientiousness with which they must be discharged, and the Altar of Incense the prayerfulness with which they must be accompanied. Nor let it be supposed that these spiritual requirements were not understood by devout worshipers, whether clerical or laical, among the Hebrews (Luke 1:10).

Withdrawing now to the inmost chamber, the Most Holy Place, which was the immediate abode of Jehovah, and excluded to all but the incumbent of the high priesthood, we find nothing therein save the Ark and its Mercy Seat, to symbolize the invisible deity: the one by the writings deposited therein, as an explicit record of moral principles; and the other by the figures standing upon it, as a conventional type of natural laws. The high priest himself is the representative of his entire order, and through it of the laity. Since the one great Day of Atonement has passed, in which Jesus as the Christian's sole High Priest has entered into the actual and immediate presence of the celestial Glory, there is no need or room for any other mediator between the soul and God (Heb. 9:11, 12, 24). The Veil is a type of His flesh (Heb. 10:20), rent at the crucifixion (Matt. 27:51), so that all saints may now enter the Holiest boldly (Heb. 10:19), clad in the regalia of Christ's own righteousness (Rev. 19:8).

THE CROWNING GLORY OF THE TABERNACLE

We conclude this part of our subject, remarking that the crowning glory of the Tabernacle and its service lay—and was universally understood as lying—in the gradual scheme of divine revelation couched under the three modes of divine manifestation, which we have been considering. Let us dwell a little longer upon them in detail.

The *Shekinah*[23] was intended merely to mark the divine abode and presence in some physical and visible manner, and conveyed no intimation of the divine purposes beyond what that simple fact implied. It manifested itself in two phases, each characteristic, and having two seemingly opposite traits: a brilliancy (significant of disclosure) and a smoke (indicative of concealment); in other words, the revelation was yet but partial.

In the "pillar of a cloud by day and of fire by night," this contrast

---

23. Late Hebrew or Chaldean *Shekináh*, lit. a *residence*, the term invented (not biblical) to describe what in the Bible is called only "the glory of Jehovah." It is spoken of as habitually "appearing" in public view on memorable occasions of divine intervention, especially in connection with the Tabernacle and other scenes in the desert, and also at the dedication of Solomon's Temple. It is distinct from the special theophanies vouchsafed to the patriarchs and prophets of Old and New Testament times, as the latter were *personal,* and the other popular. These exhibited a bodily form, more or less distinctly human, while that was merely a light. In the Transfiguration of our Savior the two aspects were blended and fulfilled.

was by alternation; the exhibit, however, was constant in one phase or the other. The object here was simply guidance in the journey, and, therefore, it was an index of the locality where Jehovah preferred His tent to be pitched, and when He wished it to be removed to some other spot. Hence it began with the first march, and ceased when the Tabernacle reached its last resting place. At the passage of the Red Sea, it changed its position from the head of the marching column to the rear, in order to interpose a barrier between the Israelites and their pursuers (Exod. 14:19, 20, 24). During the giving of the Law, it stood upon the summit of Mt. Sinai (Exod. 19:9, 16-20; 20:18-21; 24:15-18), whence it descended to the tent temporarily occupied as an office by Moses (Exod. 33:9, 10), returning to the summit of the mountain during the second interview there (Exod. 34:5). On the completion of the Tabernacle proper it took up its permanent station above the building, removing only during the march (Exod. 40:34-38). It is, therefore, the emblem of divine revelation in its lowest or general aspect of social direction in the secular or semi-ethical crises of human affairs. The ordinary hazy appearance may be compared to the quiet approval of heaven upon national or personal conduct when right. The flashes of lightning, which at times frightened beholders, may be the vindictive warnings of Providence against wrongdoing (see also p. 12).

The occasional glow over the Mercy Seat was a token of a special condescension of Jehovah, less public, but still in view of some national or ecclesiastical act of devotion. It is an emblem of the grace that prompts and rewards such an expression of religious quickening. Forlorn indeed is that state or church or individual of whose conscious center it need be inquired, "Where [is the divine] glory?" (1 Sam. 4:21.)

A more specific form of divine communication by the Almighty respecting the secrets of His administration is found in the mysterious *Urim* and *Thummim,* which, however manipulated, were resorted to only on special emergencies, chiefly public, but yet having a private bearing. They seem to correspond to the monitions of conscience in the natural heart, and to those of the Holy Spirit upon the renewed one. The two are related like the eye and light to each other, as they involved quite distinctly the subjectivity of the recipient (high priest), who acted as a medium.

Finally, we have in the *Decalogue,* treasured in the archives of the sacred Ark, the clearest and fullest code of ethics ever divulged to humanity at large, and one which all later legislation or revelation, and all modern ingenuity or science, have not materially improved nor successfully impeached. Many illustrative applications and enforcements have been added, but the moral law as expressed in those ten commandments stands unrivalled and unrepealed in every dispensation and among all except barbarous people. Few are the evils of the heart or life which their strict observance according to their true intent and spirit would not prevent or relieve.

To borrow an illustration from a science generally regarded as furnishing the most commanding and irrefragable kind of proof, we may say that, as the coincidence of two arcs, figures or planes, in three points, especially if angular, is an absolute mark of equality or identity throughout, so the correspondence in our plan of the Tabernacle with its scriptural description in the three essential elements of metric outline, utilitarian adaptation, and dignified significance, is a conclusive attestation that the value of the hitherto unknown quantities has been truly ascertained.

In order to eliminate any suspicion that even such an equation is accidental, we may further point to the fact that each of these three confirmations is itself triplicate or even compoundly so. 1. The *numerical* statements or implications as to the ground-plan, the elevations, and the roof or wall coverings respectively, however separately and independently given or deduced, precisely tally in dimension. 2. The *mechanical* adjustment of the various parts, whether expressed—sometimes in full, sometimes laconically, sometimes merely hinted,—or understood, is at once systematic, simple and efficient. 3. The *ideal import of the whole,*—from the Levitical court (with its roasting flesh), through the priestly fane (with its aromatic fumes), into the pontifical shrine (with its celestial glow). All of the details including the instructions for the construction of, and the actual use were consistent, necessary and reflective of redemptive truth. Note this: the *physical elements* (drawn from all the realms of nature), the *corporeal organisms* (animal victim, human agent, or cherubic phantasm), and the *conventional tokens* (perpetual fire in the outer court, continual light in the Holy Place, and constant shade in the Most Holy) and in the *liturgical apparatus* (whether sacrificial fixtures, or costly implements, or gorgeous paraphernalia). We submit that in every facet, this plan is admirably progressive, eminently instructive, and sublimely decorous. Nor is a single feature inconsistent, unnecessary or trivial in the entire category of details. A theory that so fully and fairly unites all the facts and principles must be sound; and in the nature of the case there can be no more convincing argument. The sacred record is the only testimony, its careful interpretation the best jurist, and common sense the highest tribunal. The ultimate verdict we are content to abide.

In conclusion, which may seem to some of our readers to savor of overweening confidence, if not of consummate egotism, it is proper to add that we are well aware of the degree of assurance with which many of our predecessors on this subject have put forth their plans of adjustment. We are sure that a number of them at least must have had secret misgivings of their sufficiency, although few have had the candor to avow (as Brown frankly does,[24]—he proceeds, it should be borne in mind, on the flat roof theory) their sense of inability to meet the requirements of the case. We have the hardihood to assert, and we are conscious of no vanity in doing so, that our only apprehension in the matter is lest our readers may hastily pass our explanations and reasons by, as ingenious and possibly plausible speculations, and may thus remain unconvinced for lack of real and thorough examination. We have no fear of their final assent (except, of course, that of the personally prejudiced, and especially of those already publicly committed to a different opinion), if they only will take the pains to verify our positions by a careful comparison with the scriptural statements and the mechanical and artistic demands of the case. To this the theme, if not the book, is fairly entitled.

---

24. Brown, W., *The Tabernacle,* p. 43.

Our difficult and somewhat venturesome task is now accomplished in as brief space as any one could reasonably demand. We think we have made out our case without any special pleading, and have, therefore, a right to subscribe, Q. E. D.[25]

---

25. *Quod erat demonstrandum* ("which was to be proved").

SCRIPTURE TEXT INDEX

The letter n *after the number indicates the reference is in the footnote.*

SUBJECT MATTER INDEX

*An asterisk * before a name indicates there are other entries under this title; the letter n after a page number indicates a footnote; the letter f after a page number indicates a Figure/illustration.*

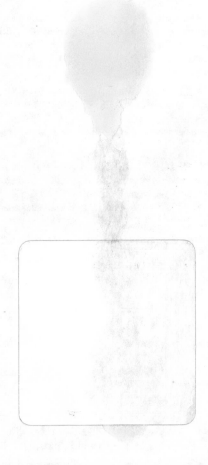